THE ORDINARY WAY

A UNIQUE WAY TO LIVE

MARK T. GOODMAN

 Five Stones Press

COPYRIGHT

99 01 435769 987123 / 001 / 7643222

Printed in the United States of America

DEDICATION

*To Vonda Kay who inspires me as we live our
everyday, ordinary lives together.
Next to my salvation through Christ,
you are my greatest gift.*

ENDORSEMENTS

God nailed Mark Goodman's heart to Alaska and he and his family have poured their lives into the people of that great state. Now, his wisdom, gained over a rich experience as an ordinary pastor in an ordinary church, is available to people everywhere who do everyday life in ordinary places unto the Glory of God.

Dr. Charles R. Wade
Pastor Emeritus of First Baptist Church Arlington, Texas

Goodman's conversation about the ordinary radiates God's extraordinary with rich Scriptural analysis and life-impacting application. Bravo!
This masterful revelation of the extraordinary within the ordinary illuminates God's Word in a way that is sure to powerfully impact lives.

Dr. Eric Ash
Wayland Baptist University

Pastor Mark Goodman is as real as they come when he encourages a revolution within our individual ordinary lives and his own life reveals the possibilities about which he writes in this book. He powerfully demonstrates the extraordinary promises of God as faithful and true when the word of God is applied to our everyday, ordinary lives. Sign me up for the revolution!

Dane Havard
Businessman

Every day we each make countless little decisions – this book inspires us to see how those choices that seem so ordinary can actually add up to a life of devotion to God and to others. Mark Goodman has provided us with a wise companion to walk with us in our pursuit of meaning and fulfillment. Reading this book redeemed the word "ordinary" for me!

Nancy Beach
Leadership Coach, Slingshot Group

God took on flesh in the person of Jesus of Nazareth. The extraordinary took on the ordinary. Mark Goodman offers practical wisdom on what it means to follow our extraordinary Savior and Lord in the ordinary things of life—a much needed reminder for believers living in a YOLO and FOMO culture.

Dr. Thomas Fuller
Beeson Divinity School

Pastor Mark T. Goodman has written an extraordinary book about living life in an ordinary way. His unique style of relating biblical truths in an easy to apply manner makes reading The Ordinary Way feel like a living room conversation about the challenges of focusing our faith walk on the beauty of ordinary. An entertaining, inspiring and memorable read, we can't recommend TOW highly enough.

Dr. Scott & Leah Silverii
Bestselling Authors

CONTENTS

PART IV

THE EXTRAORDINARY ALONG THE ORDINARY WAY

PART V

LESS THAN ORDINARY

PART VI

WORDS TO GUIDE

PART VII
SPEAK UP

INTRODUCTION

Ordinary.

That word is much underrated. Words such as *great, awesome, first class*, and *excellent* receive more attention. Few will exit the highway to grab a bite if the billboard sign reads "Ordinary BBQ" or "Home of The Ordinary Burger"—even if the sign itself is extraordinary. Why? Because *ordinary* carries synonym baggage. The word is grouped together, quite unfairly, with *boring, bland, common*, and *unimpressive*.

I officially call for a revolution. "The Ordinary Revolution," perhaps? On second thought, that doesn't sound very impressive. If you can find a better tagline, please let me know. In the meantime, that will have to suffice.

Eugene Peterson, in *The Message*, artfully articulates one of the apostle Paul's central encouragements to those who set out to follow Jesus.

So here's what I want you to do, God helping you: Take your everyday, ordinary life—your sleeping, eating, going-to-work, and walking-around life—and place it before God as an offering. Embracing what God does for you is the best thing you can do for him. Romans 12:1 MSG

In the NIV, that verse reads that we are to *offer (our) bodies as a living sacrifice.* As one who understands the powerful imagery of "living sacrifices," I, even still, struggle to apply those words. How does one actually do that? Through the ordinary. Certainly, extraordinary events hold value and excellent experiences prove worthy; the stuff of life is mostly ordinary—it is the meat that sustains rather than the gourmet feast and chocolate mousse that add flavor.

PART I

FINDING THE ORDINARY WAY

1

PINKY TOES AND AVERAGE JOES

Warning labels and orange diamond-shaped signs alert us of possible and avoidable pain and sixty-five mph panic. While not one to suggest an excess of warnings and "don't-do-this-stupid" labels, I recommend posted cautions regarding relocated furniture and carelessly placed laundry baskets.

I do not recall if I ever started a tally; if I did, I neglected counting somewhere along the way. It is next to impossible to achieve even the simplest of mathematical equations while searing pain demands attention. The collision occurs so quickly that no amount of time exists to avoid the day-altering event—that moment when the smallest of your southernmost digits collides with the solid-oak couch leg or the surprisingly sharp basket gap. Even the saintliest among us unleash long-restrained vocabulary and then proceed to the hop destined to appear on *Dancing with the Stars*. Pinky Toe, allow me to introduce you to immovable object Exhibit A. Once you commence with the one a.m. dance, you understand more the words of the apostle Paul, "If one part suffers, every part suffers with it."

Meet Joe.

His name is Joe. He lives in a middle-class neighborhood and drives a mid-sized car to a medium-wage job. During his average-length commute, Joe habitually visits the closest (never mind if it's the best) coffee hut and orders a cup of (yes, that's right) Joe—"Black, no milk or sugar, please." Joe arrives at his mid-town office, walks halfway down the hall, and places his gray bag on his middle-management desk. Today is Employee Appreciation Day. After Joe expresses appreciation to his office assistant, she informs him that the company CEO asked to see him. Joe again walks down the hall. As he approaches the boss's office, he speaks to the CFO who just departed from the office. She smiles. She feels appreciated. The CEO, just moments before, told her how thankful he was for her diligent work. Not sure what to expect, Average Joe enters the CEO's office. He sees kind eyes and a gracious smile…

Again, it will be like a man going on a journey, who called his servants and entrusted his wealth to them. To one he gave five bags of gold, to another two bags, and to another one bag, each according to his ability. Then he went on his journey. The man who had received five bags of gold went at once and put his money to work and gained five bags more. So also, the one with two bags of gold gained two more. But the man who had received one bag went off, dug a hole in the ground and hid his master's money.

After a long time the master of those servants returned and settled accounts with them. The man who had received five bags of gold brought the other five. "Master," he said, "you entrusted me with five bags of gold. See, I have gained five more."

His master replied, "Well done, good and faithful servant! You have been faithful with a few things; I will put you in charge of many things. Come and share your master's happiness!"

The man with two bags of gold also came. "Master," he said, "you entrusted me with two bags of gold; see, I have gained two more."

"His master replied, "Well done, good and faithful servant! You have been faithful with a few things; I will put you in charge of many things. Come and share your master's happiness!"

Matthew 25:14–23

Ordinary.

Pinky toes and Average Joes.

Neither spectacular, neither much noticed—both essential; both needed; both ordinary.

2

NO. REALLY. IT'S OKAY.

It's exhausting. You achieve, but not enough. You succeed, yet it's not your nation's anthem you hear. Your 3.95 is exceptional, but it's no 4.0. You don't believe it no matter how many times your friend repeats the words, "No. Really. It's okay."

You've heard another word even more times than those. You pronounce it without stutter and spell it with ease. You, however, struggle to find it no matter the depth or extent of your search.

Contentment.

The student loved his teacher. He held his mentor in highest regard. Sometimes, however, he struggled. He fought off as best he could the ever-around-the-corner desire to match, if not surpass, his teacher's success. Isn't the younger supposed to surpass the older, after all? While his mentor, Paul, wrote the words to address the temptation of love for money, Timothy still heard within them a challenge to his want for more—"contentment is great gain."

Joshua needed the reminder that his hero was dead. David's physique proved ill-suited for the first king's armor. Joshua crossed his own parted water. David slew his own giants. They found their own skin.

Timothy's travels aren't detailed on maps in the back of holy texts;

nevertheless, he served where he lived and practiced a sincere faith. He never filled Paul's shoes. He was never required to do so. He filled the ones that fit him.

A devout life does bring wealth, but it's the rich simplicity of being yourself before God.

1 Timothy 6:6 MSG

Contentment.
No, really. It's okay.
Ordinary.

3

GOOD. PERIOD.

I looked for it but to no avail, either in Genesis 1 or 2. Days one, four, and five receive a score of "good." Day three claims double that. For whatever reason, day two misses out all together; quite the opposite of day six's "very good." I looked and found no "great," "awesome," "incredible," or even "a step above."

Good. Period.

In 1995, Chris Noonan, inspired by Dick King-Smith's novel, brought to us the story of Babe. Not Ruth or a term of endearment. A pig. We see Babe corral the hapless herd of sheep and want to cry out, "Way to go!", "Awesome!" or any cry of extreme approval. However, Farmer Hoggett, so well portrayed by James Cromwell, looks to his well-trained swine friend and declares, "That'll do, pig; that'll do."

The Creator looked upon His creation and said, "That'll do." But you say, "That's not enough. Can't we add more flash, more pomp and circumstance?" No. Good. Period. "That'll do."

Perhaps our quest for more than good is part of the gross residue of sin. It's the child bound and determined to please her father and the father for whom B+ marks failure. It's the single blue ribbon not bringing enough satisfaction. It's the midlife crisis when the husband now pursues a younger love.

It's the wife for whom a best effort at home repair receives a mere nod, if any expression of appreciation at all. The quest for more than good proves endless and disheartening. Remember day seven? After six days of imagination brought to life in vivid color, expansive skies, crawling creatures, and male and female images of God, the Artist, "rested from all the work of creating that he had done."

He rested. He saw that it was very good and knew that "that'll do." Good. Period.

PART II

LIVING THE ORDINARY WAY

4

ESSENCE OF EXISTENCE

His name is forgotten or, at least, not a key element to the story. He taught and advocated for the law, the Hebrew law, expertly so. He, wanting to display his intellectual prowess, devised the most difficult exam he could muster. He approached the man named Jesus and quizzed, "Teacher, which is the greatest commandment in the Law?" (Matthew 22:36).

The GED, Bar Exam, and Thesis Defense combined! The whole enchilada! Yet even without an all-night cramming session, the Tested One blew the curve on that exam.

> *Jesus replied: "'Love the Lord your God with all your heart and with all your soul and with all your mind.' This is the first and greatest commandment. And the second is like it: 'Love your neighbor as yourself.' All the Law and the Prophets hang on these two commandments."*
>
> *Matthew 22:37–40*

Within these words Jesus summarized the essence of our existence. Yes, the Law and Prophets found their fulfillment in those few words, but so does human purpose as well. In the words of the ancient confession, humanity's purpose is "to glorify God and to enjoy Him forever."

Glorification and enjoyment find their ultimate design in the simply stated commandments of Jesus. Simply stated? Yes. Simply achieved? Not so much.

The Hebrew scholar/advocate must not have been among those gathered on the mountainside months before. You and I weren't either. We, however, can eavesdrop on the words those gathered heard. He, One who came not to abolish but to fulfill the Law and Prophets, spoke with conviction as much of the crowd absorbed the refreshing new expression of the ancient texts.

Within His words He expressed not only the truth but also the heart and intent of the divine commands. On the mountain and in other places along His journey, He gave voice to ten top priorities. "Jesus' Top Ten." We will count them down.

5

JESUS' TOP TEN—#10

Back in 1993, Jack Lemmon and Walter Matthau made America laugh as two *Grumpy Old Men*. Over three thousand years ago another grumpy old man, of sorts, made Israel fear.

The Hebrew people knew better than to laugh when Moses, their frustrated leader, dashed the two stone tablets to pieces. Thankfully, God is eternally more patient and faithful than grumpy old men and faithless followers. Whereas God provided the first two tablets, the second time around Moses had to chisel out the replacements. (Maybe Moses learned a lesson there!) In His grace, God rewrote the commandments. Those commandments served as guide and identity for the Hebrew people for over one thousand years, untouched and unaltered.

Within those commandments, Israel found their distinctiveness. As Nahum Sarna explains, unlike all other systems around them, Israel's law included life. "Life is treated holistically. It is not compartmentalized. Crime is therefore also sin" (144).

Perhaps of all Ten Commandments, #10 shows that holistic view most clearly, for as Peter Craigie states well, "the tenth is concerned primarily with motivation rather than with act" (163).

What is #10?

"You shall not covet."

Coveting is hard to prove and that is proof that God called His people to a new level of faithfulness. Don't miss the significance of that. Over three thousand years ago God set forth a law that "prohibits not just evil acts but evil desires. This is one of the most significant steps that was ever taken by any religion in history" (Shires 369).

That was a huge step, an enormously huge step indeed. But, "you ain't seen nothing yet." Something far greater is on the way; well actually, *Someone*!

"The days are coming," declares the Lord, "when I will make a new covenant with the people of Israel and with the people of Judah. It will not be like the covenant I made with their ancestors when I took them by the hand to lead them out of Egypt, because they broke my covenant, though I was a husband to them," declares the Lord.

"This is the covenant I will make with the people of Israel after that time," declares the Lord.

"I will put my law in their minds and write it on their hearts. I will be their God, and they will be my people. No longer will they teach their neighbor, or say to one another, 'Know the Lord,' because they will all know me, from the least of them to the greatest," declares the Lord.

"For I will forgive their wickedness and will remember their sins no more."

Jeremiah 31:31–34

God's words to Jeremiah highlight His message of love. God says...

- "I will make a *covenant*"
- "I took them by *the hand* to lead them"
- "I was a *husband* to them"

- "I will put *my law* in **their** *minds*"
- "and write it *on their hearts*"
- "they will *all know me*"
- "I will *forgive*"
- "remember their sins *no more*"

God does not provide His law and His covenant in order to force obedience; it is an act of love. Graeme Goldsworthy, an Australian Old Testament scholar, explains it best when he writes,

"The law is not simply a guide for human behavior; its ethics and obedience are primarily there to indicate a relationship to God. At the heart of the law is the covenant relationship with God" (156).

Twelve to fifteen hundred years after Moses and six hundred plus years after Jeremiah, the unparalleled Relationship walked into Jerusalem in the person of Jesus. The One to whom the law pointed, and of whom Jeremiah prophesied, sat down on a mountain and taught. This is how He began…

Blessed are the poor in spirit, for theirs is the kingdom of heaven.

Blessed are those who mourn, for they will be comforted.

Blessed are the meek, for they will inherit the earth.

Blessed are those who hunger and thirst for righteousness, for they will be filled.

Blessed are the merciful, for they will be shown mercy.

Blessed are the pure in heart, for they will see God.

Blessed are the peacemakers, for they will be called children of God.

Blessed are those who are persecuted because of righteousness, for theirs is the kingdom of heaven.

Blessed are you when people insult you, persecute you and falsely say all kinds of evil against you because of me. Rejoice and be glad, because great is your reward in heaven, for in the same way they persecuted the prophets who were before you.

Matthew 5:3–12

In light of these words, discovering Jesus' view of #10 is not difficult. Coveting is all about wanting. Jesus teaches, however, that God will bless those who refuse want and embrace dependence on Him.

Pay special attention to verse six. One willing to look at #10 through the eyes of Jesus will see that the only acceptable and beneficial "want" is a hunger and thirst for righteousness.

That hunger and thirst is crucial *for man does not live on bread alone* and one cannot possibly live abundantly and eternally without Jesus. Let Him explain…

Do not think that I have come to abolish the Law or the Prophets; I have not come to abolish them but to fulfill them. For truly I tell you, until heaven and earth disappear, not the smallest letter, not the least stroke of a pen, will by any means disappear from the Law until everything is accomplished. Therefore anyone who sets aside one of the least of these commands and teaches others accordingly will be called least in the kingdom of heaven, but whoever practices and teaches these commands will be called great in the kingdom of heaven. For I tell you that unless your righteousness surpasses that of the Pharisees and the teachers of the law, you will certainly not enter the kingdom of heaven.

Matthew 5:17–20

Jesus speaks those words just as He is "warming up"—just minutes into His teaching. Do you grasp the impact of His words? Hear some of them again…

For I tell you that unless your righteousness surpasses that of the Pharisees and the teachers of the law, you will certainly not enter the kingdom of heaven.

Matthew 5:20

Jesus' words here are somewhat like if I told you that if you do not grow a third leg, you will never run. Impossible, right?

That is Jesus' point exactly. He teaches His listeners that they cannot do enough to earn heaven. As a pointed and concrete example, He speaks of a group of people whom the listeners knew were the best at being "righteous"—the Pharisees. Even the Pharisees fell short! Goldsworthy skillfully and succinctly illuminates our understanding of Jesus' bold statement of impossibilities. He begins with Adam.

"The 'law' given to the first Adam, the first son of God, was broken, and mankind was thrown out of the garden into the wilderness. The law given to Israel, the son of God, was broken, and the nation was thrown out of its promised land into the wilderness of exile. A last Adam came as the truly obedient covenant partner of God, signifying his identification with a people that desperately needed his help.

We can almost hear heaven's sigh of relief, 'At last! A true son of God.' 'You are my beloved son in whom I am well pleased' is God's word of approval. Then this true Adam, this true Israel, goes out into our wilderness to be tempted and to be victorious, so that he might make for us a way back into the garden of God.

Jesus did not come to destroy or abolish the law but to fulfill it (Matthew 5:17). He is the end...of the law. He is its ultimate reference point, revealing with unprecedented clarity what Sinai was all about. He applies it with uncompromising rigidity: 'unless your righteousness exceeds that of the scribes and Pharisees, you will never enter the kingdom of heaven' (Matthew 5:20).

In the Sermon on the Mount [and] in his parable of the Pharisee and the tax collector...he takes the ground of self-justification out from under those who think they can somehow climb up the ladder of the law to acceptance with God. He has come to fulfill all righteousness for us. He not only fulfills all the law in his own sinless life, but he is content to have our law breaking imputed to him so that he bears the curse of the law for us (2 Corinthians 5:21).

By faith we receive the gift of Jesus' law keeping, which was perfectly achieved on our behalf, and in him we become the righteousness of God. By faith we do not overthrow the law: 'on the contrary, we uphold the law' (Romans 3:31). We uphold it by turning our backs on our own warped efforts to keep the law and by putting all our confidence and trust in the one who satisfies all the law's demands on our behalf' (159).

Paul, the law-lover turned Jesus-devotee, wrote on the subject. Romans 10:4 reads, *Christ is the culmination of the law so that there may be righteousness for everyone who believes.*

Again, the message is clear. If you need to want something, want Jesus and His righteousness.

Number 10 is crucial to follow in your life because if you covet, you will miss out on contentment and the blessing of being "blessed."

Probably all of us know a child who is never satisfied—one who, no matter what he has, always wants more. Truth be told, those childhood habits die hard. Maybe it's a nicer car or a bigger house or a larger salary or a different spouse or someone else's success or another's life— What do you want that you do not need? Be careful!

On another day of teaching Jesus, as was His habit, told a story about a farmer who planted his seeds in different types of soil. In the story, the seeds are the words of God and the soils are different hearts and minds of people in whom those words are planted. As you heed the caution to avoid coveting, listen to Jesus' explanation of part of that story.

...the desires for other things come in and choke the word...
   Mark 4:19

Those words ring in our ears and bruise our souls.
As we look at #10 through the eyes of Jesus, I see two options.
Option Number One:

Ignore #10. Commit yourself to always wanting more. Spend large amounts of time thinking about the cool stuff that belongs to your neighbor. Dedicate your life to accumulating all that you desire and achieving the highest roles of success.

Option Number Two:

Adopt #10. Commit yourself to viewing the fields of lilies so that you will know that God loves you more than these. Spend large amounts of time thinking about God's promise to "watch over the way of the righteous." Dedicate your life to hungering for all that God is ready to give and thirsting for the kingdom of heaven."

If you are wondering, I suggest option number two.

6

JESUS' TOP TEN—#9

When the One who boldly states, "I am the way and the truth and the life" (John 14:6) speaks, I know that it is a good idea to listen. For that reason, we continue in this chapter to examine Jesus' Top Ten List. That is, we are taking a look at the Ten Commandments as Jesus taught them when He taught His followers how He fulfilled the Law over one thousand years after Moses climbed the mountain to receive it from God.

The well-known commandments are true and rich; however, to understand their full meaning, we need to see them as Jesus did. Martin Luther, the great Protestant reformer, agreed as he wrote,

"As thunder without rain did more harm than good; so Ministers, that preach the terrors of the law, but do not, at the same time, drop in the dew of gospel instruction and consolation, are not 'wise master-builders;' for they pull down, but build nothing up again" (qtd. in Bridges 238).

As a pastor, my aim at all times is to build others up in the knowledge and grace of God. I aim to do that in this chapter as together we view Jesus' Top Ten.

Number 10 was "You shall not covet." So, what is #9?

You shall not give false testimony against your neighbor.
  Deuteronomy 5:20

While the specific intention of this law addressed falsehood spoken during a legal dispute, it is quite clear that we are staying within the nature of the law when we condense #9 to "You shall not lie."

We saw that coveting deals more with desire or motivation rather than an act. Number 9, however, deals primarily with an act, which, by the way, can be driven by #10. At first glance, as a matter of comparison, you may wonder why God included #9 in a list of commandments that, from human perspective, seem much more serious than lying. But then again, we take another look and then remember some of the damage lies have caused. Here are but a few...

Jacob drove his brother away.

Joseph's brothers sent their father into mourning.

Peter fell from faithfulness.

Ananias and Sapphira fell down and died.

Nations waged war.

Nixon resigned.

Clinton obstructed justice.

Felicity Huffman bought her daughter's way into college

And here is another...

You lost someone's trust.

The prophet Isaiah described God as *one true God* (Isaiah 65:16), and Jesus stated Himself that He is *the truth* (John 14:6). Therefore, it is evident that God does not condone lying. The author of Proverbs drives the point home somewhat more firmly.

There are six things the Lord hates, seven that are detestable to him: haughty eyes, a lying tongue, hands that shed innocent blood, a heart that devises wicked schemes, feet that are quick to rush into evil, a false witness who pours out lies and a person who stirs up conflict in the community.

Proverbs 6:16–19

Two out of the seven things that the Lord detests deal with lying. That's 28.5 percent!

Thus far I have written about Jesus yet I have not referred to the New Testament to examine His view of #9. Let's check that out together. First, go back to that great sermon that Jesus shared on the mountain.

> *Again, you have heard that it was said to the people long ago, "Do not break your oath, but fulfill to the Lord the vows you have made." But I tell you, do not swear an oath at all: either by heaven, for it is God's throne; or by the earth, for it is his footstool; or by Jerusalem, for it is the city of the Great King. And do not swear by your head, for you cannot make even one hair white or black. All you need to say is simply "Yes" or "No"; anything beyond this comes from the evil one.*

> *Matthew 5:33–37*

In those first few verses, Jesus deals with what today we know as "I swear"; "pinky swear"; and "cross my heart, hope to die." Why is it that we feel the urge to make sure others know we are telling the truth? Because sometimes we *aren't* telling the truth. Jesus raised the bar on truth-telling by telling His listeners that a "yes" should really mean yes. You may have heard your father or grandfather say, "I remember when a deal was sealed with a handshake." If the world followed #9, we would not need notaries.

Do you recall the 28.5 percent? Well Jesus, the Son of God and Word of God, is consistent with the Father in His disgust of lying. In fact, He let a group of religious leaders "have it" because they forgot the importance of truthfulness. I like Eugene Peterson's version of those words.

> *You're hopeless! What arrogant stupidity! You say, "If someone makes a promise with his fingers crossed, that's nothing; but if he swears with his hand on the Bible, that's serious." What ignorance! Does the leather on the Bible carry more weight than the skin on your hands?*

And what about this piece of trivia: "If you shake hands on a promise, that's nothing; but if you raise your hand that God is your witness, that's serious"? What ridiculous hairsplitting! What difference does it make whether you shake hands or raise hands? A promise is a promise. What difference does it make if you make your promise inside or outside a house of worship? A promise is a promise. God is present, watching and holding you to account regardless.

Matthew 23:16–22 MSG

Backing up to Matthew chapter 5, did you notice Jesus' reason for staying with a simple "Yes" or "No"? He said, "anything beyond this comes from the evil one" (Matthew 5:37). What is the lesson? Well if you recall, Isaiah called God *one true God*. Compare that description to Jesus' summary of the evil one.

When he lies, he speaks his native language, for he is a liar and the father of lies.

John 8:44c

A commitment to telling the truth marks a determination to embrace #9 and follow the *one true God* rather than the father of lies.

Remember the words of Graeme Goldsworthy from the last chapter, "The law is...primarily there to indicate a relationship to God...the covenant relationship with God" (156).

I cite that again to emphasize that word *relationship*. God loves you and created you to love Him and to love others. Jesus made that abundantly clear in the Great Commandment. With that in mind, we also know that a lie to God or from one person to another does great damage to those divine and human relationships—even one "little" lie.

"Well it took the hand of God Almighty

To part the waters and the sea.

But it only took one little lie

To separate you and me.

Oh we are not as strong as we think we are"
(Mullins, verse 1).

Truly we are not as strong as we think we are and we struggle with embracing #9. Yet *if we will* and *when we do* embrace #9, we will restore relationships, primarily our relationship with God.

One clear and beneficial way to evaluate your progress on #9 is to ask yourself and others what they see in you. Do they—do *you*—see integrity?

"I desire so to conduct the affairs of this administration that if at the end, when I come to lay down the reins of power, I have lost every other friend on earth, I shall at least have one friend left, and that friend shall be down inside of me."

— *ABRAHAM LINCOLN*

Dr. Charles R. Wade, my friend and pastor, writes, "The root meaning of the word 'integrity' is 'to be whole.' Wholeness is based on truth" (292). Wade continues,

"…transparency and truth help keep us pure, and they are among the most precious gifts we can bring to others. Tell the truth" (292).

With certainty, you have had and will have times when you struggle to tell the truth. However, in order to embrace #9, you need to discover that even when the immediate results may be a challenge and painful, the end result is a pure heart and no regrets.

Listen to the experience of an athlete who told the truth. Ruben Gonzalez was playing against Marty Hogan in the third stop of the 1985–86 RMA Pro Tour.

"The match was capped with one of the most stunning displays of sportsmanship ever seen on the men's tour. With Hogan serving at match point and Gonzalez trailing by only two, Ruben ended a furious rally with a mid-court forehand kill, called good by referee Corey Brysman.

Instead of stepping up to serve, however, Gonzalez overturned the call himself saying the shot had skipped and offered his hand to Hogan in congratulations. It was a courageous act which cost Gonzalez the only real shot he has ever had at winning a major tour event" (Stoddard).

When asked why he did it, Ruben said, "It was the only thing that I could do to maintain my integrity. I could always win another match, but I could never regain my lost integrity" (qtd. in Curtis).

Tell the truth; you will be glad you did.

7

JESUS' TOP TEN—#8

The powerful and succinct words of the Old Testament prophet Micah tell us how to live.

> *He has shown you, O mortal, what is good. And what does the Lord require of you? To act justly and to love mercy and to walk humbly with your God.*

Micah 6:8

Not living up to his namesake, Micah Whitaker, the Alaska resident, was sentenced to five years in prison for mail fraud—cashing stolen checks. In 2001, US retailers reported that shoplifters cost them twenty-five million dollars a day. Just a few years ago I discovered, by viewing my credit card statement, that I had purchased hundreds of dollars of dental equipment in Indonesia.

As a son and son-in-law of dentists, I found my unbeknownst act of charity rather ironic. In 2009, we learned that a former Miss Alaska and Rhodes Scholar was not wise enough to avoid defrauding institutions of large amounts of loans and scholarships.

Clearly a great number of people failed to receive the word on #8 of Jesus' Top Ten.

What is #8? "You shall not steal."

The Hebrew word there for steal is *ganah*. The corresponding Greek word, sounding awfully familiar, is *klepto*.

Some are fond of stealing!

Perhaps it is the thrill of risk or perhaps the desperation of need. Perhaps it is the enticement of greed or the "keeping up with the Joneses," or even the joy of impressing peers. Whatever the reason, #8 still stands as a rule of law that, as we will see, Jesus broadened to the call to love.

Even before Jesus widened the scope of "You shall not steal," Moses transcribed in stone the law that God spoke to enrich the people of Israel; it was not to hinder. Professor Pierson Parker explains the importance of the gift of #8. He writes, "As Israel advanced from the nomadic to the agricultural and urban stages, property became more and more a social concern" (368).

In a gathered community of the Hebrew people, theft greatly affected their unity. One such example occurs in Joshua, chapter 7. Israel, by then a mighty fighting force, loses what should have been an easy victory. God reveals to Joshua, their leader, the cause of the defeat... Theft! Upon investigation a man named Achan is confronted. Listen to Achan's response.

Achan replied, "It is true! I have sinned against the Lord, the God of Israel. This is what I have done: When I saw in the plunder a beautiful robe from Babylonia, two hundred shekels of silver and a bar of gold weighing fifty shekels, I coveted them and took them. They are hidden in the ground inside my tent, with the silver underneath."

Joshua 7:20–21

Please take note of two words in verse 21: "I coveted." Number 8 is much easier to follow when you attend to #10.

Earlier I said that Jesus widened the scope of "You shall not steal." Let's take a look.

And if anyone wants to sue you and take your shirt, hand over your coat as well. If anyone forces you to go one mile, go with them two miles. Give to the one who asks you, and do not turn away from the one who wants to borrow from you.

Matthew 5:40–42

Jesus raises the bar! He challenges the common understanding of keeping #8. He calls His followers to go several steps further than refraining from theft. He says that if someone takes your shirt (the inner garment), give them, in addition, your coat (the outer garment). Modern translation: "If someone steals your shirt, give them your North Face coat as well."

The demand is stronger than we at first observe. D. Martin Lloyd-Jones, author and minister, explains that under Jewish law at the time, a person "could never be sued for his outer garment, though it was legitimate to sue for the inner one" (283). Give them more than the law requires.

Now we *do* see examples in Scripture, even in the life of Jesus, of persons being rightly brought before the law and receiving just punishment. Obviously we do not need to understand these words as a call never to engage the law or to allow crime and abuse to stand. However, our motive should never be to use the law or any other means to avenge our anger or to "destroy" the life of another so that we can feel justified.

Ben Witherington aptly states that, "Self-sacrifice replaces self-interest as the fundamental basis of ethics in the Dominion of God…" (137). The fundamental basis of Jesus' ethic was and is self-sacrifice. The prophet Isaiah foretold the response of Christ to others robbing Him of "life and limb."

He was oppressed and afflicted, yet he did not open his mouth; he was led like a lamb to the slaughter, and as a sheep before its shearers is silent, so he did not open his mouth.

Isaiah 53:7

As we continue with our focus on #8, let me draw your attention to a master of presenting theology in practicality. The apostle Paul, the one blinded, reborn, and commissioned by the radiant Christ, knew how to combine the Old Testament (Hebrew Scriptures) and the teachings of his Lord Jesus, forging them into a call to believers to see the bigger picture so that they (and we) could discover obedience, driven by grace. Hear his words.

Let no debt remain outstanding, except the continuing debt to love one another, for whoever loves others has fulfilled the law. The commandments, "You shall not commit adultery," "You shall not murder," "You shall not steal," "You shall not covet," and whatever other command there may be, are summed up in this one command: "Love your neighbor as yourself." Love does no harm to a neighbor. Therefore love is the fulfillment of the law.

Romans 13:8–10

"Love your neighbor as yourself" rings a loud and not too strange bell. The Scriptures and their message remain consistent. See page 9. See, also, Leviticus 19. The literal translation of the final phrase of verse 10 reads, "The fullness of the law, therefore, is love."

By obeying #8, you are well on your way to living as Christ called you to live—a life devoted to love.

Professor Gerald Cragg challenges us to see the far-reaching effect of love as it pulses through our veins, fed by our heart. He writes, "If we really love another person, we cannot possibly injure him in any of the suggested ways. Love would stifle at birth the thoughts which lead to adultery, murder, theft, or any form of covetousness" (606).

"Stifle at birth." What a phrase!

John 21 records the resurrected Christ asked His frustrated disciple, "Simon son of John, do you love me?"

And not just once.

Simon Peter thought he loved Jesus until he discovered by Christ's call that love stifles all self-interest and selfish protection. Jesus summarized love to Peter with two phrases:

"Feed my sheep." and "Follow me!"

To follow #8, we will need to know Jesus, love His sheep, and follow Him where He leads. He leads us into the way of love. It is a good thing to be stifled, stifled by love, for love to stifle—

- Your greed
- Your thrill of unhealthy risk
- Your desperation of need
- Your keeping up with the Joneses
- Your joy of impressing your peers

Love stifle on.

8

JESUS'S TOP TEN—#7

Two months following his thirty-seventh birthday, a pastor submitted himself to soldiers who arrested him and led him to Tegel military prison. If you, like Dietrich Bonhoeffer, were held by Nazi guards for two years, how would you spend your time in prison?

In addition to serving as pastor to fellow prisoners, Bonhoeffer devoted much of his time to writing. These thoughtful and deeply theological letters and papers continue to captivate modern readers. In the prison camp, however, Bonhoeffer's focus of writing covered more than pastoral theology alone. Surrounded by threat and death, Bonhoeffer wrote a sermon for his niece, Renate Bethge, and her fiancé, Eberhard. Read on for excerpts from the pastor-uncle.

A wedding sermon from a prison cell written in 1943
   —Dietrich Bonhoeffer

"It is right and proper for a bride and bridegroom to welcome and celebrate their wedding day with a unique sense of triumph. When all the difficulties, obstacles, hindrances, doubts, and misgivings have been, not made light of, but honestly faced and overcome...then both parties have indeed achieved the most important triumph of their lives. With the 'Yes' that they have said to each other, they have by their free choice given a new direction to their lives... Every wedding must be an occasion of joy that human beings can do such great things, that they have been given such immense freedom and power to take the helm in their life's journey.

God today adds His 'Yes' to your 'Yes.'

Marriage is more than your love for each other. It has a higher dignity and power, for it is God's holy ordinance. ...

It is not your love that sustains the marriage, but from now on, the marriage that sustains your love.

God makes your marriage indissoluble. *'What therefore God has joined together, let no man put asunder' (Matthew 19:6)*...[Y]ou can now say to each other with complete and confident assurance: We can never lose each other now; by the will of God we belong to each other till death.

[It is] a sign of social disintegration when the wife's service is felt to be degrading or beneath her dignity, and when the husband who is faithful to his wife is looked on as a weakling or even a fool.

Don't insist on your rights, don't blame each other, don't judge or condemn each other, don't fault with each other, but accept each other as you are, and forgive each other every day from the bottom of your hearts.

The right beginning and daily practice are very important indeed.

From the first day of your wedding till the last the rule must be: 'Welcome one another... for the glory of God'.

That is God's word for your marriage. Thank Him for it; thank Him for leading you thus far; ask Him to establish your marriage, to confirm it, sanctify it, and preserve it. So your marriage will be 'for the praise of His glory'. Amen" (qtd. in Schwedes).

Why would a pastor/theologian devote prison-sentence time to writing marriage reflections? Because he wanted to help his niece set off in the right direction and because he knew how often men and women either set off in the wrong direction or lose the map somewhere along the journey.

Long before the twentieth-century German pastor provided part of the marriage map, the Almighty provided protective truth to keep us from steering off the road. That protective truth of which I speak is #7 in Jesus' Top Ten.

What is #7? "You shall not commit adultery."

Take note of the obvious: #7 is included in the Ten Commandments. Its inclusion in the Ten adds force by asserting that "adultery…involved not only unfaithfulness to the other partner, but also unfaithfulness to God" (Craigie 160). We will see that when Jesus taught, He raised the bar on this commandment. Yet even before the first-century Messiah taught, the Almighty also raised the bar for as Peter Craigie explains, in other cultures "adultery…was primarily a secular offense" (160).

Adultery not only grieves the heart of the betrayed spouse, it grieves the heart of God.

The bold and truth-speaking prophet Nathan confronted David, King of Judah, with his sin. To the king, Nathan spoke these words, "Why did you despise the word of the Lord by doing what is evil in His eyes?" (2 Samuel 12:9).

God, the Almighty, spoke through the brave prophet right into the heart of Judah's king. Pierced and full of shame, David pleaded with his Creator. We have the words that he expressed. He turned his prayer of contrition into lyrics to a psalm. Hear his plea:

Have mercy on me, O God, according to your unfailing love; according to your great compassion blot out my transgressions. Wash away all my iniquity and cleanse me from my sin. For I know my transgressions, and my sin is always before me. Against you, you only, have I sinned and done what is evil in your sight; so you are right in your verdict and justified when you judge. Surely I was sinful at birth, sinful from the time my mother conceived me. Yet you desired faithfulness even in the womb; you taught me wisdom in that secret place. Cleanse me with hyssop, and I will be clean; wash me, and I will be whiter than snow. Let me hear joy and gladness; let the bones you have crushed rejoice. Hide your face from my sins and blot out all my iniquity. Create in me a pure heart, O God, and renew a steadfast spirit within me.

Psalm 51:1–10

God heard his sincere cry for mercy and the Lord of grace extended forgiveness.

That's David's story. Moving from the king of BC, we push forward to the King of AD, specifically, the first century AD. We climb up the hillside again and find a seat at the feet of the King as He speaks His message that began with the beautiful and worldview-changing words, "Blessed are the poor in spirit." We arrive just as He turns His attention (and captures ours) to His expansion of the seventh commandment. Jesus says:

> *You have heard that it was said, "You shall not commit adultery." But I tell you that anyone who looks at a woman lustfully has already committed adultery with her in his heart. If your right eye causes you to stumble, gouge it out and throw it away. It is better for you to lose one part of your body than for your whole body to be thrown into hell. And if your right hand causes you to stumble, cut it off and throw it away. It is better for you to lose one part of your body than for your whole body to go into hell.*

Matthew 5:27–30

In these words of Jesus we see the breadth of #7 through His eyes and the difficulty of finding anyone who has *not* committed the sin of adultery within their heart.

- second looks
- imaginative romance
- lustful longing
- pornography
- consumed thought

While not everyone who partakes of these internal longings succumbs to the external actions, many do. The pain and "fallout" of such action leaves its mark.

Guard yourself against breaking #7 by heeding the words of Jesus. Craig Blomberg provides the challenge. In his words: "Christians must recognize those thoughts and actions which, long before any overt sexual sin, make the possibility of giving in to temptation more likely, and they must take dramatic action to avoid them" (109).

Fleshing out those final words of wisdom, I would like to equip you with four actions to avoid adultery.

Four Adultery-Avoiding Actions:

1. Marry For More Than Love.

The beginning of the sentence first spoken by Jesus and oft repeated in weddings states, "Therefore what God has joined together..." (Mark 10:9a). Love is great grounds for marriage, but you will start well if your foundation goes deeper than the dirt. Read again some of Bonhoeffer's words of charge to his Renate and Eberhard.

"Marriage is more than your love for each other. It has a higher dignity and power, for it is God's holy ordinance. ...

It is not your love that sustains the marriage, but from now on, the marriage that sustains your love" (qtd in Schwedes).

Do not try on marriage only to later redress as the fashions and styles change.

2. Avoid False Expectations.

Louis Evans, Jr. comes forward with the costs of marriage. The costs of privacy, of self-centered scheduling, and of individualistic economics. After counting the costs, however, Evans writes, "But oh, what value there is in that which is precious" (243).

Too often couples, young and perhaps old as well, enter into matrimony not so holy because they bring in the baggage of false expectations. If you listen to "love songs" of yesterday and today, you hear promises and statements such as:

- "You are the air I breathe."
- "You are the center of my life."
- "I will swim the seas for you."
- "You are the light of my life."

Those may fit well on Hallmark cards, but they do not sustain marriages. You cannot give all your spouse needs, nor should you expect that from your spouse. Particularly, do not attempt to plug voids with your spouse that only God can fill.

3. Don't Neglect the "Have and Hold."

The apostle Paul, who himself encouraged singlehood for believers, recognized the value of intimacy in marriage.

Now for the matters you wrote about: "It is good for a man not to have sexual relations with a woman." But since sexual immorality is occurring, each man should have sexual relations with his own wife, and each woman with her own husband. The husband should fulfill his marital duty to his wife, and likewise the wife to her husband. The wife does not have authority over her own body but yields it to her husband. In the same way, the husband does not have authority over his own body but yields it to his wife. Do not deprive each other except perhaps by mutual consent and for a time, so that you may devote yourselves to prayer. Then come together again so that Satan will not tempt you because of your lack of self-control.

1 Corinthians 7:1–5

Most newlyweds need no reminder to love their spouse physically. Nevertheless stress, commitments on the road, time unwisely spent, past hurts, and even children find a way of building a barrier between the two who are meant to live as one flesh. Guard against this barrier by "having and holding" each other. Within marriage sexuality and intimacy are not shameful; no, rather they are a gift of God.

. . .

4. Remember Your Vows.

I want you to hear two paragraphs that I speak as a charge to each and every couple for whom I perform their wedding ceremony.

"As the two of you are married, it will be important for you to remember God's instructions for marriage. If marriage were always easy, it would not be a commitment. You will have to be open and honest with each other. You will have to share your deepest joys and pains.

God designed marriage to last a lifetime. He has entrusted you both with this holy commitment. God has done a wonderful thing by bringing you together, and He expects great things from those He loves. The promises you make today are not temporary; they are to last and carry through all that life brings. Whenever laziness or greed or temptations try to weaken your bond, you must trust in God, trust in each other, and remember the vows you speak today."

Please pay close attention to that last sentence. "Whenever laziness or greed or temptations try to weaken your bond, you must trust in God, trust in each other, and remember the vows you speak today."

In our society, men die for honor and many fight for their honor through word and deed. Some of the causes are worthy and some are merely fueled by pride. If you are going to stand up for honor, please stand up for honor in your marriage. That is a worthy cause.

Dr. Calvin Miller writes:

"I am much afraid that those with other definitions of love are often forced to admit on the very porches of divorce courts that their biggest moments of love were somewhere back around their honeymoons. After that the greatness of all they called love shrinks into transactions and mechanics. Someone mows, someone does the laundry, and both go to bed wishing for five real minutes of conversation that says something is still left of their marriage vows. And the 'dear' becomes 'drear.' And the drear dwindles down to an uninteresting finish.

I know now that when you mean your promise and feel its glory, you have truly become a lover, for besides honor there is no other porch before that grand house called love" (206–07).

Avoid adultery by constructing a well-built porch. You do that by meaning your promise and feeling its glory.

9

JESUS' TOP TEN—#6

In this chapter we reach the halfway mark. In our countdown to number one in Jesus' Top Ten, we have reached number six. So far, numbers ten to seven presented their call for us to flee from…

- Coveting
- Lying
- Stealing
- Adultery

What is #6? "You shall not murder."

Of all ten, this commandment appears to be the easiest to follow. Yet before we check off the "completed" box by #6 and move on to the next, we need to pay heed to the words of D. Martin Lloyd-Jones when he writes, "It is possible for us to face the law of God as we find it in the Bible, but so to interpret and define it, as to make it something which we can keep very easily…" (223).

Whether it is selective reading or hearing, it will not do.

With Old Testament eyes, we can view "You shall not murder" as one easily followed. While several translations of the Bible use the word "kill," others, including the NIV, use the more specific word "murder." As J. Coert Rylaarsdam wrote, "It forbids all killing not explicitly authorized" (986).

While that is true, we know just how true, as well, is the old adage: Give a man an inch and he'll take a mile.

Those persons led by Moses who first received the Ten Commandments found support from them as they formed community. They discovered, through negative experience, that "murder is not a private affair, for it weakens the whole society to which the victim belonged," as Pierson Parker expressed (367). Murders produce fear, uncertainty, disunity and much more. While they looked to laws such as #6 to protect their unity, they failed to see, as we also often do, that following the letter of the law falls far from adequate.

Just how far from adequate does it fall?

To answer that question, we must put in our New Testament contacts to provide clearer vision for our currently Old Testament focused eyes. We are, after all, counting down *Jesus'* Top Ten! We respect Moses, but we follow Jesus! Our specific, vision-improving contacts will come from Jesus' great sermon on the hillside, a sermon often visited in our countdown.

> *You have heard that it was said to the people long ago, "You shall not murder, and anyone who murders will be subject to judgment." But I tell you that anyone who is angry with a brother or sister will be subject to judgment. Again, anyone who says to a brother or sister, "Raca," is answerable to the court. And anyone who says, "You fool!" will be in danger of the fire of hell.*

Matthew 5:21–22

Just as we are about to check the "completed" box, Jesus says with all authority, "But *I* tell you." What? Did He say there is more to #6 than refraining from murder? Am I not off the hook? Clearly Jesus, yet again, raises the bar. In addition to upholding the ban on murder, He adds at least two other restrictions:

1. Anger
2. Name-calling

Two Restrictions:

1. Anger

Tryon Edwards wisely said, "He who can suppress a moment's anger may prevent a day of sorrow" (qtd. in Jenkins 16). Unfortunately, we all know the sorrow of anger. We need to release it to God in order to free ourselves from the grip of its bondage.

We would all acknowledge the wrongfulness of anger; yet, of what do we speak when we use that word? I well remember a discussion/debate (or quiet argument) in which a couple of junior high classmates and I engaged during art class. (Respect for teachers may be the topic for another book!)

The two argued that Jesus sinned during His cleansing of the temple by turning over the tables of the money changers. I, at the time, somewhat the arrogant defender of the faith, quoted 1 Peter 2:22 which says, "He committed no sin." After quoting Peter, I debated the validity of "*righteous* anger."

While I believed Scripture and spoke in such a manner as to match that belief, I was not as sure internally that I understood the difference between righteous anger and all other types. C. S. Lewis writes of Jesus' call to love our neighbor and to forgive our enemies: "That is what is meant in the Bible by loving him: wishing his good, not feeling fond of him nor saying he is nice when he is not" (108).

Jesus did not sin. We do. There will be times when your anger is "righteous" and acceptable, but those times are the exception. The other cases of less-than-righteous anger find avenues for negative expression. J. Edgar Park wrote, "murder never accomplishes anything except to work off the irritation or fury of the moment" (986).

In agreement with Park, I add that irritation and/or fury themselves do great harm to self and others even when, in most cases, they do not lead to murder. We need to place a personal restriction on our anger.

In addition, we need the restriction of…

2. Name-calling

Jesus spoke in more than generalities. He said that saying *Raca* to another or by calling another a fool puts one in danger of the "fire of hell." Those are firm words, to say the least. Why did Jesus speak in such a way? It helps to realize the substance of the words. *Raca*, an Aramaic word, means *empty-headed* or we might say *idiot*. And the phrase *You fool* is rather self-explanatory.

Nevertheless, a further look at the original language in which these words were written reveals that the Greek word for *fool* is *moros*. From that word, we derive the English word *moron*. Receiving the title *moron* always injures. Additional words of Jesus explain why name-calling hurts Him so.

- "Love your neighbor as yourself." (Matthew 22:39)
- "Love one another. ...By this all men will know that you are my disciples." (John 13:34–38)
- "I pray...that all of them may be one." (John 17:20–21)

I enjoy spending the day with my kids—Kate, Max, and Sam. During our time together one day, I observed an action that seemed rather foolish, to which I responded, "That was a stupid thing to do." Without hesitation, my then-eight-year-old spoke for the Holy Spirit as she asked, "Daddy, is stupid a nice word to say?"

In a feeble attempt to justify myself, I explained to her that I did not call the person stupid, but rather called the act stupid. Conviction already set in and it was too late. You see, my wife, Vonda Kay, and I teach our children kindness and love. In that moment, I failed as the teacher of kindness and love and so my Lord got ahold of me through my daughter. Thank You, God! Thank you, Kate!

Truly, Jesus raised the bar on #6. Warren Wiersbe said it best in his book, *Be Loyal*. He explains Jesus' bar-raising: "[Jesus] made a fundamental change without altering God's standards: He dealt with the attitudes and intents of the heart and not simply with the external action" (37).

As you strive to follow #6, allow the Spirit of God to work on and change your attitudes and intents. The Spirit's work will keep you from committing premeditated murder, murder through action, and murder through anger and name-calling.

10

JESUS' TOP TEN—#5

Today when we think of ham, we picture a tasty lunch meat or that meat which sweet pineapple slices and cherries top with beauty and taste. However, when Moses sat down to write about Ham in the first book of Hebrew Scripture, he thought of one of the three sons of Noah. Listen to a story about Ham, the man not the lunch meat!

The sons of Noah who came out of the ark were Shem, Ham and Japheth. (Ham was the father of Canaan.) These were the three sons of Noah, and from them came the people who were scattered over the whole earth. Noah, a man of the soil, proceeded to plant a vineyard. When he drank some of its wine, he became drunk and lay uncovered inside his tent. Ham, the father of Canaan, saw his father naked and told his two brothers outside. But Shem and Japheth took a garment and laid it across their shoulders; then they walked in backward and covered their father's naked body. Their faces were turned the other way so that they would not see their father naked.

When Noah awoke from his wine and found out what his youngest son had done to him, he said, "Cursed be Canaan! The lowest of slaves will he be to his brothers." He also said, "Praise be to the Lord, the

God of Shem! May Canaan be the slave of Shem. May God extend Japheth's territory; may Japheth live in the tents of Shem, and may Canaan be the slave of Japheth."

Genesis 9:18–27

Ham learned the hard way that it is not wise to laugh at another's expense, especially when that other is your father.

In this chapter we continue our countdown to number one in Jesus' Top Ten. We come to number five.

What is #5? "Honor your father and mother."

When we study the Ten Commandments, we observe that God calls us to faithfulness in all areas of life including society's basic unit, the family. We all understand that healthy families lead to healthier communities. Community health benefits all societies, the Hebrew people of the Old Testament included. Particularly in a community like that of the nomadic Israelites, the unity of families strengthens the group as a whole. God made this clear.

In the chapter preceding the Deuteronomical listing of the Decalogue we find a word to parents that calls them to a way of living, parenting, and teaching.

Only be careful, and watch yourselves closely so that you do not forget the things your eyes have seen or let them fade from your heart as long as you live. Teach them to your children and to their children after them. Remember the day you stood before the Lord your God at Horeb, when he said to me, "Assemble the people before me to hear my words so that they may learn to revere me as long as they live in the land and may teach them to their children."

Deuteronomy 4:9–10

Keep his decrees and commands, which I am giving you today, so that it may go well with you and your children after you and that you may live long in the land the Lord your God gives you for all time.

Deuteronomy 4:40

With those words, God gave the parents in the Hebrew nation their call to commitment in parenting. With the words of #5, God gave the children of those parents their call. Since #5 is a word to children, you may think I should make this the topic of a chapter directed to children. However, we dare not limit the definition of children to infants through high school seniors. As Pierson Parker wrote, "we recognize that the commandment is (first) addressed to adult males" (367).

With number five, God spoke to children, regardless of the age of their parents.

Most children leave "the nest" eventually; and while some return, even those that don't must hear and heed the call to honoring their parents.

Jesus, the eternal Son, understood the importance of honoring parents.

1. Jesus honored Mary.

On the third day a wedding took place at Cana in Galilee. Jesus' mother was there, and Jesus and his disciples had also been invited to the wedding. When the wine was gone, Jesus' mother said to him, "They have no more wine."

"Woman, why do you involve me?" Jesus replied. "My hour has not yet come."

His mother said to the servants, "Do whatever he tells you."

Nearby stood six stone water jars, the kind used by the Jews for ceremonial washing, each holding from twenty to thirty gallons.

Jesus said to the servants, "Fill the jars with water"; so they filled them to the brim.

John 2:1–7

Although Jesus spoke a word to Mary pointing to His higher purpose, He nevertheless answered His mother's request. In his book *The Real Mary* Scot McKnight writes:

"However we explain the end of the wine supply, Mary's observation that the wine was gone was filled with expectation that Jesus *should* fix the problem. We don't know what Mary expected— did she expect Jesus to perform a miracle? Did she expect him to inform the guests so they might not get unruly? We don't know. Details aside, it is clear that Jesus understood his mother's words as carrying an honor code, fifth-commandment-claim-as-a-mother on him to do something about the wine" (65).

2. Jesus honored His Father.

Speaking to the Jews who questioned Him, Jesus said, "I honor my Father" (John 8:49 NAS).

John 5:19: "Jesus gave them this answer: "Very truly I tell you, the Son can do nothing by himself; he can do only what he sees his Father doing, because whatever the Father does the Son also does."

Knowing that the Lord, Savior, and Christ honored His mother and Father, you will better understand why Jesus voiced His displeasure with Pharisees who found an honoring loophole. Listen to His words.

And why do you break the command of God for the sake of your tradition? For God said, "Honor your father and mother" and

"Anyone who curses their father or mother is to be put to death." But you say that if anyone declares that what might have been used to help their father or mother is "devoted to God," they are not to "honor their father or mother" with it. Thus you nullify the word of God for the sake of your tradition. You hypocrites! Isaiah was right when he prophesied about you:

"These people honor me with their lips, but their hearts are far from me. They worship me in vain; their teachings are merely human rules."

Matthew 15:3b–9

The wisdom literature of Proverbs declares in chapter 20, verse 20 that, "Anyone who curses father and mother extinguishes light and exists benighted" (MSG).

The Pharisees displayed their benighted state through the practice on which Jesus calls their hand, a practice called Qorban. Qorban was a loophole through which the Pharisees could dedicate food, money, and property to God and the temple, which in actuality amounted to filling their own pockets. "Sorry, Mom, I would help you afford a place to stay, but I gave that money to God." "Dad, I would like to help with the groceries, but, as you know, I need to buy that fatted calf for my sacrifice."

Michael Wilkins explains the issue at hand: "The Pharisees and teachers of the law perform religious rituals externally, but their primary motivation has not been to commit their entire inner person to God" (536).

As it applies to the honoring of your parents, what areas of your life and actions need more internalization? External presentation is not enough. Take Father's Day, for example. If you made a call or bought a gift for your dad, did you share a word of honor and love with it?

When I gave my "groom's speech" during our rehearsal dinner, I spoke of my parents' influence in my life. Better at sermons than groom's speeches, I said, while meaning more, that my parents "did the best they could" raising me. While not said in the way I intended, I did not do a good job honoring my parents. Have you honored your parents lately?

In his book *The Year of Living Biblically*, A.J. Jacobs tells of his efforts to do so.

"I don't treat them nearly well enough. I honor them only in a lip-service way. I call them every weekend, but I spend the twenty minutes of the phone call playing hearts on my PowerBook or cleaning the closet while tossing out the occasional 'mm-hmmm.' I delete without reading my mom's emailed jokes...And when I do reply to her emails, I often do the I'm-so-important-I-don't-have-time-to-capitalize-or-punctuate thing.

So in this biblical year, I've been on a mission to reform. I've been trying to capitalize my emails to my mom. And to actually listen to what my parents say during our weekly calls. Listening is a key theme in the Scriptures" (242).

When parents and children live in a manner worthy of the call which God places on them, the family is enriched and their understanding is broadened. Theodore Wedel wrote that:

"Obedience in a Christian family...does have meaning. Obedience here can be in the Lord. Children in a Christian family soon become conscious of the fact that the obedience asked of them is not based upon arbitrary power, but upon a higher law to which the parents themselves are subject" (730).

Regarding Wedel's words on Christian families, it is right to ask about those families where the parents are not Christians or they do not behave in a Christian manner. Unfortunately some parents, both those who claim Christ and those who do not know Him, do not live in a way that is honorable.

With that reality in mind, think back to the Ten Commandments. God spoke those to a people and during a time in which children often were viewed as property. To provide a command to honor demonstrates God's love that elevates the value of each person. *Property* does not decide to honor; *people* do!

There are indeed situations where children, regardless of age, need to reject the words and/or actions of their parents. In his words on the

Ephesians passage calling children to obedience, F. F. Bruce buffers the call with the following words:

"In such a situation the law of Christ would have to take precedence even over parental orders, but in a spirit of love, not of defiance, since the law of Christ is the law of love" (165).

Without hesitation, I will say that there is a Parent eternally worthy of honor. Follow the lead of Jesus and honor the Father of heaven and earth. If you don't, He will ask you why you neglect to do so.

"A son honors his father, and a slave his master. If I am a father, where is the honor due me? If I am a master, where is the respect due me?" says the Lord Almighty.

"It is you priests who show contempt for my name.

But you ask, 'How have we shown contempt for your name?'

Malachi 1:6

As you follow #5 with your parents, give great honor to your Creator, your Father.

JESUS' TOP TEN—#4

Often when I asked our children where they would like to go to lunch, Sam voted for Chick-fil-A. Since we do not have that particular restaurant in Alaska, our home, we now pick other places. Sam requested that restaurant when we lived in Texas. We often enjoyed a bike ride and lunch at our local Chick-fil-A. Tim Hawkins, also from Texas, shares our liking of the "fil-A." In fact, he dedicated a song to Chick-fil-A. Check it out on YouTube.

To Hawkins' chagrin, the famous chicken restaurant continues to stand by the practice Truett Cathy established in 1946 when he founded Chick-fil-A. You will not find one of his eating establishments open on a Sunday. Why such a practice?

On their website you can hear the answer directly from Truett Cathy's son or you can listen to Truett himself in the form of his autobiography.

"Chapter 5—Observing The Fourth Commandment

When Saturday came during our first week of business back there in 1946, Ben and I sank exhausted into a couple of chairs after the dinner crowd had thinned. Between the two of us, we had covered six twenty-four-hour shifts.

'What do you think, Truett?' my brother asked.

'I think we ought to close tomorrow,' I replied.

The thought of working around the clock on Sunday and then starting all over again on Monday was just too much. From then on, we told customers, 'We're open twenty-four hours a day, but not on Sunday.'

Closing on Sunday has become a distinctive principle of my Christian background. From my infancy, my Sunday school teachers and pastors stressed that Sunday is the Lord's Day. I see another reason. God commanded. 'Six days you shall labor and do all your work' (Exod.20:9). God told the Israelites to work only six days so that the seventh could be used for rest.

God blessed the seventh day and sanctified it, set it aside. The book of Genesis describes the seventh day as a very, very special day. It is made for man, not man for it.

While I was growing up, Sunday was an important day for family times together; often Mom and Dad would take us to visit kinfolks. I believe God gave His laws not to make life hard but to make it better. Our bodies and our minds need time off to recharge. I've accepted that as a principle and honored God by doing it. God has honored us and the business because of it.

How could I teach the thirteen-year-old boys in my Sunday school class to observe the Lord's Day if my cash registers were jingling at my restaurants?

Although we've been closing my places of business for more than forty years, I keep hearing the same comments and questions:

'Look at all the business you're losing.' That's the most common one. I don't believe we've lost any sales in the long run. In the shopping malls where we locate our Chick-fil-A restaurants, we usually generate more sales per square foot in six days than many others do in seven.

We also believe that by giving employees that free day, we attract the kind of people who want Sunday off because of their own convictions. People who take a day of rest to worship the Lord and to refresh themselves spiritually and physically are the kind of associates we seek" (69–70).

Leading his company in a direction guided by personal conviction, Truett Cathy displays deed-matched belief. He believes in following the example set by the Creator, the example of taking time to rest.

What is #4 in our countdown of Jesus' Top Ten? "Observe the Sabbath day."

The noun *Sabbath* comes from the Hebrew verb *shabbat*, which means "to cease." Ceasing is not an easy practice for most Americans who Kris Haig identifies as a people suffering with the "addiction of productivity." And as with any addictive behavior, one who tries to overcome compulsive productivity will experience withdrawal. To this, Rev. Barbara Brown Taylor writes:

"Most of us are so sold on speed, so invested in productivity, so convinced that multitasking is the way of life that stopping for one whole day can feel at first like a kind of death.

As the adrenaline drains away, you can fear that your heart has stopped beating since you cannot hear your pulse pounding in your temples anymore. As you do no work, you can wonder if you are running a temperature since being sick is the only way that you ever get out of work. As time billows out in front of you, you can have a little panic attack at how much of it you are wasting since time is not only money but also the clock ticking on your life."

While a prime minister, a genius, and a US President all advocated "power naps," we often grant our respect to those who "burn the candle at both ends." Nevertheless Winston Churchill, Albert Einstein, and George W. Bush are not men most would consider as lazy. Other world leaders and great minds, however, have adopted a life without rest.

So it is clear to see that ceasing from work is not a topic on which people agree, even in the church.

"The early leaders of the Christian church gave no sanction to the idea that Sunday was the heir of the Sabbath, but in the lay mind there was always a sense of some connection between the two observances, and this feeling was legalized in AD 789 by Charlemagne's decree which forbade all ordinary labor on Sunday as a breach of the Fourth Commandment.

The reformers of the sixteenth century definitely stated that the

Fourth Commandment was abrogated by the N.T., yet human nature requires a day of rest from labor, so, they felt, we cannot do better than follow the tradition which sets apart the first day of the week for worship and rest. The result of this stand was that there was a decided slackening in Sunday observance, so that in the seventeenth and eighteenth centuries Protestantism turned back to the O.T. for authority in enforcing Sabbath observance" (Park 984).

As has been our practice throughout these chapters devoted to Jesus' Top Ten, when we seek answers to difficult questions, we look to Jesus. This time, however, let's begin by reading the commandment as given by God through Moses.

> *Observe the Sabbath day by keeping it holy, as the Lord your God has commanded you. Six days you shall labor and do all your work, but the seventh day is a sabbath to the Lord your God. On it you shall not do any work, neither you, nor your son or daughter, nor your male or female servant, nor your ox, your donkey or any of your animals, nor any foreigner residing in your towns, so that your male and female servants may rest, as you do. Remember that you were slaves in Egypt and that the Lord your God brought you out of there with a mighty hand and an outstretched arm. Therefore the Lord your God has commanded you to observe the Sabbath day.*

Deuteronomy 5:12–15

In this passage, God gives His people two reasons for keeping or observing the Sabbath. We find an additional reason in Exodus 20.

Reasons for Sabbath:

1. To remember God's power and provision. One author reminds us that, "The constant need to work, shop, and meet demands can be a practical denial that God is 'in control'" (*Take Back Your Sabbath*, 42).

2. To recall that while they once were slaves, they are now free.

3. (In Exodus) To follow the example of God's rest (as seen in Genesis 2).

God provided double the manna for the nomadic Israelites in the desert on Sabbath eve so they could rest on the Sabbath day. God loved His people and gave them the gift of a day of rest. Yet, as is far too often still the case, His people turned His gift into their burden.

The teachers of the law and the elite Hebrew leaders of the first century AD observed the Sabbath. In their observance, however, they turned the positively stated commandment into another, "Thou shall *not!*" They replaced the heart of the law with the heavy burden of requirements. As they walked around in pomp and circumstance, stage right, Jesus entered the scene.

One Sabbath Jesus was going through the grainfields, and as his disciples walked along, they began to pick some heads of grain. The Pharisees said to him, "Look, why are they doing what is unlawful on the Sabbath?"

He answered, "Have you never read what David did when he and his companions were hungry and in need? In the days of Abiathar the high priest, he entered the house of God and ate the consecrated bread, which is lawful only for priests to eat. And he also gave some to his companions."

Then he said to them, "The Sabbath was made for man, not man for the Sabbath. So the Son of Man is Lord even of the Sabbath."

Another time Jesus went into the synagogue, and a man with a shriveled hand was there. Some of them were looking for a reason to accuse Jesus, so they watched him closely to see if he would heal him on the Sabbath. Jesus said to the man with the shriveled hand, "Stand up in front of everyone."

Then Jesus asked them, "Which is lawful on the Sabbath: to do good or to do evil, to save life or to kill?" But they remained silent.

He looked around at them in anger and, deeply distressed at their stubborn hearts, said to the man, "Stretch out your hand." He stretched it out, and his hand was completely restored. Then the Pharisees went out and began to plot with the Herodians how they might kill Jesus.

Mark 2:23–3:6

How did their view of Sabbath get so skewed that they went from complaining about disciples picking grain to plotting on how to kill Jesus? William Lane mourns their lack of understanding and lack of love when he writes:

"In the name of piety they had become insensitive both to the purposes of God and to the sufferings of men... As Lord of the Sabbath Jesus delivers both the Sabbath and man from a state of distress" (123–124).

In the name of piety, the Pharisees would have preferred the disciples go hungry and the hand of the man remain shriveled.

In his telling of an event much like this one, Luke throws out a stinging word describing the religious leaders' actions; words which, when I read, literally make me want to weep.

Indignant because Jesus had healed on the Sabbath, the synagogue leader said to the people, "There are six days for work. So come and be healed on those days, not on the Sabbath."

Luke 13:14

Jesus, stirred by righteous anger, looked that synagogue ruler in the eyes and spoke His indignation declaring, "You hypocrites!" Yet, His righteous anger is so much different from our selfish anger for He still loved those hypocrites. Hear Jesus' words from later down the road.

As he approached Jerusalem and saw the city, he wept over it...
Luke 19:41

God is still weeping. He weeps for you, He weeps for me, when we take one of His gifts and turn it into a burden. I mentioned before that more than a few opinions on Sabbath observance exist. That is important to know because we can turn gifts into burdens when we force our views upon others.

One person considers one day more sacred than another; another considers every day alike. Each of them should be fully convinced in their own mind. Whoever regards one day as special does so to the Lord. Whoever eats meat does so to the Lord, for they give thanks to God; and whoever abstains does so to the Lord and gives thanks to God. For none of us lives for ourselves alone, and none of us dies for ourselves alone. If we live, we live for the Lord; and if we die, we die for the Lord. So, whether we live or die, we belong to the Lord.

Romans 14:5–8

With these guidelines for refraining from judgment in mind, we continue in our study of Sabbath so that we can formulate how and when we will receive God's gift of rest.

Sabbath-keeping Considerations:

1. Jesus reaffirmed the truth of Sabbath.

Jesus never told His disciples or His critics to cease Sabbath. Rather, He pointed back to the heart of the Sabbath. Matthew includes a statement that Jesus spoke which Mark does not record. It comes in the same context—the grain-picking disciples and the shriveled hand; and it is worth hearing. Jesus said, *I desire mercy, not sacrifice* (Matthew 12:7).

2. Jesus rested during His ministry.

- *Jesus often withdrew to lonely places and prayed* (Luke 5:16).
- *Jesus went out to a mountainside to pray, and spent the night praying to God* (Luke 6:12).

- Jesus rested and taught resting in faith.

Therefore I tell you, do not worry about your life, what you will eat or drink; or about your body, what you will wear. Is not life more than food, and the body more than clothes? Look at the birds of the air; they do not sow or reap or store away in barns, and yet your heavenly Father feeds them. Are you not much more valuable than they? Can any one of you by worrying add a single hour to your life?

Matthew 6:25–27

Notice what Jesus practiced and taught. While we know He slept, as He did on the boat, for Jesus, Sabbath and true rest involved reflection on and time spent with God, the Father.

3. Jesus rose on a New Sabbath.

In Acts 20:7, the earliest history of the church, we read that the believers in and followers of Jesus met and worshipped on the first day of the week. Why Sunday now and not Saturday? Why the first day now and not the seventh? Peter Craigie answers with this explanation:

"The relationship expressed between the Sabbath and the Exodus in this commandment is directly analogous to the relationship between the Lord's Day (Rev. 1:10; the first day of the week) and the resurrection of Jesus Christ in the Christian faith.

The Exodus, marking the liberation and 'creation' of a new people, was linked to the Sabbath; the Exodus had been the redemption of Israel by their God from slavery (Exod. 15:13). Likewise, the resurrection of Jesus Christ marked liberation from an old life and entry into a new life, which was the gift of God in love (See Eph. 2:4–10). Thus, for the Christian, the principle of the fourth commandment remains in force, though the day has been changed" (158).

As far as we can tell, John, the disciple, was the first to give the New Sabbath a new name. In his foreword to the revelation of God that he shares, John reports that God's Spirit spoke to him "on the Lord's Day" (Rev. 1:10). The Lord's Day—what a good name!

God gave former slaves the gift of a day for rest and worship. Jesus called His followers to rest in Him.

By the way, at the time of his death in 2014, Truett Cathy's fortune had reached 6.3 billion dollars ("S. Truett Cathy," Forbes). Closing shop for one day a week for the purpose of physical, emotional, and spiritual rejuvenation has by no means hurt the company's "bottom line."

For God's sake, take a break!

12

JESUS' TOP TEN—#3

A tired yet determined man walks among sheep that, while not his own, he treats with care and protection. In just a matter of moments the careful shepherd once surrounded by sheep finds himself surrounded by the glory of God.

In that glorious moment, the Almighty promotes the leader *of sheep* to serve as the leader *of His people*. In order to encourage His hand-picked servant and to show His power and authority, the Almighty grants Moses the hearing of His Name. This is what Moses heard:

"*'Ehyeh-Asher—'Ehyeh.*"

"*I Am Who I Am.*"

Allow the impact of God's identity to sink in. Who but God is simply, yet profoundly, "*I Am*"?

In the words of Thomas Browne, "Indeed [God] only *is*; all others have been and shall be" (qtd in Park 875).

God, as seen in His name, cannot be pushed into the past nor forced far into the future. While involved in days-gone-by, God does not belong to them. While fully aware of and in control of the future, God is not relegated to the days-to-come.

After He boldly spoke "I Am," He continued with another name of identification. Moses hears: Exodus 3:15.

God also said to Moses, "Say to the Israelites, 'The Lord, the God of your fathers—the God of Abraham, the God of Isaac and the God of Jacob—has sent me to you.' This is my name forever, the name you shall call me from generation to generation."

Notice the title, *"The Lord."* That is the English translation of the Hebrew Tetragrammaton YHWH (a.k.a.: Adonai or Jehovah). At the age of eighty, Moses received the call of the Lord (Yahweh) to lead His people. To point to God's sovereignty, it is worth noting a prophetic name eight decades before his call. Moses' mom's name was *Jochebed.* Her name means "Yahweh is glory." At Moses' birth, his mother's name already bore the name that Moses would hear from God on the mountain!

Nahum Sarna speaks to this fact. He writes: "The first biblical personage to bear a name compounded of a divine element derived from [the] Tetragrammaton is fittingly, Jochebed, mother of Moses" (52).

Some will say, "What's in a name?" Much, especially when it comes to God.

In our Top Ten countdown, what is #3? "You shall not misuse the name of the Lord your God."

Tossing the name of God around like a cheap beach ball is not a new habit only seen in our day. From near the beginning of time, men and women have used God's name...

- As a magic formula
- As a name lifted with prayer toward worthless purpose
- By linking His name to selfish purpose (Craigie, 156)
- As a word for frustration relief
- For a cheapened expression of excitement

It was also used for the sake of less-than-sincere vows. Earl Kalland explains that the first hearers of the third commandment hear a restoration on using the Divine name. Kalland writes:

"The Israelites were not to use the Lord's name to seal such declarations in a light or frivolous manner or without the intention of fulfilling the oath, vow, or promise" (54).

How often have you said, "I swear to God" without such intention?

Fast-forwarding from the Old Testament Israelites to the New Testament teachings of Jesus, we see the Savior's words as to #3. The One who said let your yes be yes and your no be no upheld the honor of His Father's name. Listen to His rather familiar words with that in mind.

> *This, then, is how you should pray:*
>   *"Our Father in heaven,*
>   *hallowed be your name,*
>   *your kingdom come,*
>   *your will be done,*
>   *on earth as it is in heaven.*
>   *Give us today our daily bread.*
>   *And forgive us our debts,*
>   *as we also have forgiven our debtors.*
>   *And lead us not into temptation,*
>   *but deliver us from the evil one."*

Matthew 6:9–13

If you grew up in a tradition that voiced this prayer often, maybe even on a weekly basis, you may hear these words in such a rote way that you miss their meaning. In regard to #3, focus on the meaning of one particular phrase: "Our Father in heaven, *hallowed* be your name" (emphasis mine) is worthwhile.

God is holy and pure. So also is His *name*. R. T. France writes: "This clause…is not merely a petition…but is itself an expression of that reverence which his holiness requires" (246).

Scripture "forbids the idle or empty use of God's name" (Wright, 366).

Within the Jewish tradition, they often write the name of The Holy as such...*G_D*. Out of respect for their Creator, they will not spell out His name fully. They honor and uphold the name of God.

The apostle Paul did, also—as reflected in one of the most beautiful works of poetry ever written.

> *In your relationships with one another, have the same mindset as Christ Jesus:*
>
> *Who, being in very nature God, did not consider equality with God something to be used to his own advantage; rather, he made himself nothing by taking the very nature of a servant, being made in human likeness. And being found in appearance as a man, he humbled himself by becoming obedient to death—even death on a cross!*
>
> *Therefore God exalted him to the highest place and gave him the name that is above every name, that at the name of Jesus every knee should bow, in heaven and on earth and under the earth, and every tongue acknowledge that Jesus Christ is Lord, to the glory of God the Father.*

Philippians 2:5–11

In the closing stanza, Paul calls followers of Christ to hallow the name of Jesus. That respect does not belong to the Father alone.

A reflection on history to discover the call for such honor will help. During a time span of the third to the first century BC, Hebrew scholars, in a desire to bring the Sacred Text to more ears, took on the grand task of translating Hebrew Scripture (Old Testament) into Greek. That early translation is known as the *Septuagint*, or *LXX* for short. When they came to the Exodus text where God identifies Himself to Moses as "I Am," the scholars translated the Hebrew language into the Greek "*ego eimi.*"

About thirty to forty years after they translated those words, Jesus had a conversation with some of the Jewish leaders, perhaps some of those same scholars.

"Are you greater than our father Abraham? He died, and so did the prophets. Who do you think you are?"

Jesus replied, "If I glorify myself, my glory means nothing. My Father, whom you claim as your God, is the one who glorifies me. Though you do not know him, I know him. If I said I did not, I would be a liar like you, but I do know him and obey his word. Your father Abraham rejoiced at the thought of seeing my day; he saw it and was glad."

"You are not yet fifty years old," they said to him, "and you have seen Abraham!"

"Very truly I tell you," Jesus answered, "before Abraham was born, I am!"

John 8:53–58

The accusers attempted to relegate Jesus to the present. He was not yet fifty years old. How could He claim fellowship with Abraham, the father of their faith? Jesus explains with these words, *"before Abraham was born, **I am!**"*(emphasis mine).

The Greek words for "I am" are *"ego eimi."*

When I write of the Triune God (the Father, the Son, and the Spirit), I write of the One who is "I Am." I write of the One who *was*, who *is*, and who is *to come.* Such a supreme God deserves respect, reverence, and awe.

Love for God moves one to reserve His holy name for speaking to Him and for speaking about Him. *His* name is *above all names* and no other name holds such *power.*

This, then, is how you should pray:
　　"Our Father in heaven,
　　hallowed be your name,
　　your kingdom come,

71

your will be done,
on earth as it is in heaven.
Give us today our daily bread.
And forgive us our debts,
as we also have forgiven our debtors.
And lead us not into temptation,
but deliver us from the evil one."

The Lord's Prayer—Matthew 6:9–13

13

JESUS' TOP TEN—#2

Have you ever noticed or experienced the difficulty of breaking a habit? Habits relish in holding on. One such latching-on habit that grips humankind is the practice of reversing Genesis 1:27.

So God created mankind in his own image, in the image of God he created them; male and female he created them.

Unfortunately men and women, through their actions, often rewrite Scripture to read: "So *man* created God in *his* own image."

In this chapter we give attention to #2 in our countdown to #1. We look at the Ten Commandments through the eyes of Jesus. In rewriting Genesis 1:27, we neglect #2.

What is #2? "You shall not make for yourself an idol."

You shall not make for yourself an image in the form of anything in heaven above or on the earth beneath or in the waters below. You shall not bow down to them or worship them; for I, the Lord your God, am a jealous God, punishing the children for the sin of the parents to the third and fourth generation of those who hate me, but showing love to a thousand generations of those who love me and keep my commandments.

Deuteronomy 5:8–10

Obviously, religion predates Moses; however, expressing the Word of God, Moses proclaimed a distinct monotheist faith.

"One of the major themes of biblical literature is the struggle against paganism... It is the arrival of Moses on the scene of history that heralds the first appearance of the notion of a war on polytheism... The Ten Commandments clearly and unambiguously mandate the absolute prohibition on polytheism and idolatry for the entire people of Israel...This strict and comprehensive formulation demands the exclusive recognition of and allegiance to one God, the One who showed Himself to be active in history and who is known to Israel by the name that is consonantally written in Hebrew YHVH" (Sarna 144–145).

Take note of that final word—*YHVH* (YHWH). We discussed the power and significance of that Holy Name in the previous chapter. God alone exists in such unique and unmatched form, thus bearing an unequaled name. God, the Great I Am, *is*! All else flows from Him. In light of this belief, while most Christians keep what I am calling #1 and #2 distinct, the Hebrew people combine those commandments. In other words, because there is no other god but God, they are not to make idols.

When we read the idol-making prohibition, we come to discover two restrictions.

Two Restrictions:
  1. No idols as gods.

You saw no form of any kind the day the Lord spoke to you at Horeb out of the fire. Therefore watch yourselves very carefully, so that you do not become corrupt and make for yourselves an idol, an image of

*any shape, whether formed like a man or a woman, or like any animal
on earth or any bird that flies in the air, or like any creature that
moves along the ground or any fish in the waters below. And when
you look up to the sky and see the sun, the moon and the stars—all the
heavenly array—do not be enticed into bowing down to them and
worshiping things the Lord your God has apportioned to all the
nations under heaven. But as for you, the Lord took you and brought
you out of the iron-smelting furnace, out of Egypt, to be the people of
his inheritance, as you now are.*

Deuteronomy 4:15–20

When you understand the call of God, particularly in verse 19, you
see that God wants us to *enjoy* nature. He says "*when* you look up at
the sky...*all* the *array*" (emphasis mine). God says, go ahead; take a
good long look—check out what I made for you and Me to enjoy. Yet,
don't let that long look lead to worship of nature, the creation. Give
your awe and honor to Father God, not "Mother Nature." God created
the world. That truth stands in opposition to pantheism, the belief that
"everything in nature is divine" (Erickson 123).

2. No idols for God.

The words of Scripture cast great imagery describing God. They
call for devotion to God not the images, however.

God is Father, but not the same as your dad.

God is King, yet no earthly throne encapsulates His glory.

God is Shepherd, but not limited to the pasture.

God is Lamb, yet He deserves more than an "ah" received by cute
sheep.

God is Lion, but no "king of the beasts" roars as loud as the King
and Creator of that small kitty-cat.

No image stands in for God; for as Peter Craigie writes, "the image
may become the thing that is worshipped, and this would detract from
the proper kind of worship which was a response of love" (154).

The initial people who received the call to reject idol-making sometimes did a good job (see Daniel 3); sometimes they did a poor job.

> *Then he said to Jeroboam, "Take ten pieces for yourself, for this is what the Lord, the God of Israel, says: 'See, I am going to tear the kingdom out of Solomon's hand and give you ten tribes. But for the sake of my servant David and the city of Jerusalem, which I have chosen out of all the tribes of Israel, he will have one tribe. I will do this because they have forsaken me and worshiped Ashtoreth the goddess of the Sidonians, Chemosh the god of the Moabites, and Molek the god of the Ammonites, and have not walked in obedience to me, nor done what is right in my eyes, nor kept my decrees and laws as David, Solomon's father, did.'"*

1 Kings 11:31–33

History continued and the pattern continued: good job, poor job, good job, poor job, etc. By the time of the first century AD, just as the Father prepared to send His Son, the Hebrew people reserved their worship for God (YHWH), so it seemed. But a problem remained. A twentieth-century Scottish pastor writes:

"In external appearance, indeed, it might have seemed as if progress had been made instead of retrogression. The nation was far more orthodox than it had been at many earlier periods of its history. Once its chief danger had been idolatry; but the chastisement of the Exile had corrected that tendency forever, and thenceforward the Jews, wherever they might be living, were uncompromising monotheists... But, in spite of all this religiosity, religion had sadly declined...during four hundred years no prophet's voice had been heard. The records of the old prophetic utterances were still preserved with almost idolatrous reverence..." (Stalker 34–36).

For the most part, the images and models of animals, poles, and mythological heroes were removed. However, words and tradition quickly filled the space they vacated.

Into that world, the only image of God worthy of such worship appeared.

The Word became flesh and made his dwelling among us. We have seen his glory, the glory of the one and only Son, who came from the Father, full of grace and truth.

John 1:14

The Son is the image of the invisible God, the firstborn over all creation.

Colossians 1:15

The incarnate Christ brought divine image to a people whose eyes failed to see; He shed light on the identity of YHWH, the God of Abraham, Isaac, and Jacob, to the Creator. Joseph and Mary as well as weary and frightened shepherds held the Infant and saw God. The Word became flesh!

For our day and our sake, I am grateful that Jesus came to earth before the days of digital cameras, or Polaroids, for that matter.

Jesus did no posing or modeling. Jesus, although the image of God, did not concern Himself with image. No one needs to know what Jesus looked like in order to love Him. No image does Him justice. Rather than have us *look*, He prefers for us to *listen*.

Even one who did see Jesus in the flesh learned this lesson.

And he said to them, "Truly I tell you, some who are standing here will not taste death before they see that the kingdom of God has come with power."

After six days Jesus took Peter, James and John with him and led them up a high mountain, where they were all alone. There he was transfigured before them. His clothes became dazzling white, whiter than anyone in the world could bleach them. And there appeared before them Elijah and Moses, who were talking with Jesus.

Peter said to Jesus, "Rabbi, it is good for us to be here. Let us put up three shelters—one for you, one for Moses and one for Elijah." (He did not know what to say, they were so frightened.)

Then a cloud appeared and covered them, and a voice came from the cloud: "This is my Son, whom I love. Listen to him!"

Suddenly, when they looked around, they no longer saw anyone with them except Jesus.

As they were coming down the mountain, Jesus gave them orders not to tell anyone what they had seen until the Son of Man had risen from the dead.

Mark 9:1–9

The furthest thing from Peter's mind was idolatry, yet Jesus corrected His disciple's desire to capture Jesus in one place for worship. Jesus is too glorious and majestic to be confined to a tent! If Jesus granted Peter the freedom to build those shelters, throngs of people would have climbed that high mountain. There is something within each person that will not find contentment in letting the mystery of God remain a mystery.

"God is absolutely sovereign precisely because He is wholly independent of the world He created, and He does not inhere in it. To represent an invisible God in any material and tangible form whatsoever is by definition to distort the divine reality. It compromises God's absolute transcendence. If God is said to be also immanent in the world, that is to say, if God is not withdrawn from the human arena but is present in the life of the world, it means that His presence is attested to by the impact of His personality on the human scene, not by a visible material representation" (Sarna 145).

With no assistance from an idol needed, a young summer camper years ago grasped the image of God. To my wife, the elementary girl said: "God is so Big!" She captured the right image.

Rediscover the mystery of God; reconnect with the magnitude of the Creator!

14

#1

10, 9, 8, 7, 6, 5, 4, 3, 2...

In this chapter we reach #1 in our countdown of Jesus' Top Ten. Number one proves worthy of its top spot. Without #1, 10 through 2 fall flat. Number one gives the reason, purpose, and motivation for observing each of the other nine.

As an introduction to his declaration of the Ten Commandments to the people of Israel, Moses reminded them of a grand fact..."The Lord our God made a covenant with us" (Deuteronomy 5:2).

A covenant is an "I–Thou" commitment. In order for "thou" (you and I) to respond with gratitude and obedience to the eternal "I" (God), we need to embrace the covenant as a gift to which we commit our lives. We do a disservice to the gift of God's law if we view it as red tape restrictions. God's law is love. God establishes this through His preface to the great Decalogue.

Deuteronomy 5:6—"I am the Lord your God, who brought you out of Egypt, out of the land of slavery."

With these words, God identifies Himself as their God ("your

God") and as the One who set them free ("brought you out of Egypt"). G. Ernest Wright's words bring delightful clarity to the power of God's words. He writes, "God is *first* known as *Savior*, only secondarily as Lawgiver and Judge" (364).

When we see God first and foremost as Savior, we grasp the love within the law. As one commentator explains:

"...the law becomes the instrument of a mutual relationship in which faith responds to love. This transforms the law into a form for expressing gratitude" (Rylaarsdam 980).

In our Top Ten, we see that #1 points us to the best expression of gratitude we can voice and hold to.

What is #1?

"You shall have no other gods before me."

Far too often humans replace the true God with false, yet easily accessible, gods. These gods call out for attention and too often receive that which they crave.

When I talk with individuals about a relationship with Christ the Savior, I always direct their attention to the profound and clear words of Romans 10:9. Take a look at that Declaration of Faith.

"Jesus is Lord."

Take another look...

"_____ is Lord."

That blank begs to be filled. You and I need to fill that spot with Jesus, the Lord of lords and King of kings. However, the draw to give Jesus' spot to another person, thing, or passion proves strong.

In a sermon that he preached over fifty years ago pastor, scholar, and civil rights leader Martin Luther King, Jr. provided the great antidote to giving God's place to another. That antidote is a proper understanding of the power of God. Here are a few of King's piercing yet encouraging words.

"At the center of the Christian faith is the conviction that there is a God of power who is able to do exceedingly abundant things in nature and in history. This conviction is stressed over and over again in the Old and New Testaments. The God whom we worship is not a weak and incompetent God. God is able to beat back gigantic waves of opposition and to bring low prodigious mountains of evil. This ringing testimony of the Christian faith is that God is able...

At times we may feel that we do not need God, but on the day when the storms of disappointment rage, the winds of disaster blow, and the tidal waves of grief beat against our lives, if we do not have a deep and patient faith our emotional lives will be ripped to shreds. There is so much frustration in the world because we have relied on gods rather than God.

We have genuflected before the god of science only to find that it has given us the atomic bomb, producing fears and anxieties that science can never mitigate. We have worshipped the god of pleasure only to discover that thrills play out and sensations are short lived. We have bowed before the god of money only to learn that there are such things as love and friendship that money cannot buy and that in a world of recessions, stock market crashes, and bad business investments, money is a rather uncertain deity. These transitory gods are not able to save us or bring happiness to the human heart. Only God is able. It is faith in God that we must rediscover."

Just to what does King call his audience? To *trust* God. When you trust God, you will not replace Him.

A few thousand years after God spoke #1, the Hebrew people continued to uphold this necessary monotheistic belief.

There indeed is *one* God.

Jesus agreed with the Hebrew people; yet to them, it did not appear as such. In the beginning of John's gospel, we read those profound words as to Jesus' identity.

John 1:1—In the beginning was the Word, and the Word was with God, and the Word was God.

John wrote those words as he was inspired by God to do so. He also wrote those words because He believed the statements of Jesus that He spoke about Himself. Words such as these...

My sheep listen to my voice; I know them, and they follow me. I give them eternal life, and they shall never perish; no one will snatch them out of my hand. My Father, who has given them to me, is greater than all; no one can snatch them out of my Father's hand. I and the Father are one."

Again his Jewish opponents picked up stones to stone him, but Jesus said to them, "I have shown you many good works from the Father. For which of these do you stone me?"

"We are not stoning you for any good work," they replied, "but for blasphemy, because you, a mere man, claim to be God."

John 10:27–33

Out of respect of commandment #1, the Jews picked up rocks. Even in the presence of angry men with rocks ready to throw, Jesus spoke the truth. He boldly proclaimed that in order to uphold #1, they must see that He was (and is) God. We understand that and define that as Trinitarian theology.

There is one and only one God. The eternal One, the eternal Three-in-One, calls for our devotion. Before Him, you shall not have any other god.

Other gods attempt entry in our lives.

- god of pleasure
- god of security
- the god of "all paths are equal"
- the god of inclusiveness

One of the things which Jesus taught and the Scriptures continue to proclaim is the unique place of God. God will not settle for shared worship. He calls for your all, not a sample.

No one can serve two masters. Either you will hate the one and love the other, or you will be devoted to the one and despise the other. You cannot serve both God and money.

Matthew 6:24

Again Jesus speaks of exclusive devotion. He cautions, *Whoever is not with me is against me* (Matthew 12:30).

The apostle Paul would not have his hearers and readers confused on the subject of Christ's identity. While Jesus was Man, He was not merely man. Give heed to these words…

The Son is the image of the invisible God, the firstborn over all creation. For in him all things were created: things in heaven and on earth, visible and invisible, whether thrones or powers or rulers or authorities; all things have been created through him and for him. He is before all things, and in him all things hold together. And he is the head of the body, the church; he is the beginning and the firstborn from among the dead, so that in everything he might have the supremacy. For God was pleased to have all his fullness dwell in him, and through him to reconcile to himself all things, whether things on earth or things in heaven, by making peace through his blood, shed on the cross.

Colossians 1:15–20

The One who is before all things came to dwell with His creation so that we would know the love of God. He fulfilled the covenant of law with the covenant of love. The One who is before all things deserves your exclusive worship.

A very simple question helps reveal the exclusivity of one's worship. Before what or whom do you genuflect?

The good answer is to *bow* before the Triune God who is One and discover the power to live the Top Ten.

Live for the Triune God who is One and discover life's purpose.

Believe in the Triune God's unique and unsurpassed identity and find true identity.

Trust in the Triune God who is One and discover that God is able.

15

#ELEVEN?

Perfect ten! Ten out of ten! Thus go the expressions and evaluations of beauty, athletic achievement, and academic pursuits. Something about ten deserves an "Amen!" Or perhaps a less "churchy" "Right on!"

Seven days in a week. Good. Twelve tribes. Good. Twelve disciples. Good. Three Amigos. Good. Jesus' ten. Good. Sure the math proves easier; but more importantly, there is no more to say. Jesus, in responding to the arrogant teacher and providing counsel to the mountain climbers, said enough. Ten giving flesh to two. Enough said.

Good.

PART III

THE ORDINARY WEEK

16

INTRODUCTION

The "Top Ten of Jesus" stands the test of time. He set forth the call to follow Him and provided the map for the journey by means of His words of instruction. Journeys occur one step at a time. Steps—or swimming strokes!

Ben Lecomte's journey began in September of 2015 on the shores of Tokyo. He entered the chilly waters of the Pacific Ocean and headed east toward San Francisco. In an interview with staff of National Public Radio on August 23, 2015, Lecomte explained his approach, one that carried him across the Atlantic in 1998. He said, "I never jump into the water thinking about the entire ocean, I just cut into small pieces."

You have your own adventures and endeavors that most likely don't include swimming distances of over five thousand miles; nevertheless, Lecomte's words can help. You have a journey before you called "Life." The best way to travel that journey is by cutting it into small pieces. Take life one day at a time. One ordinary day at a time.

Sunday, Monday, Tuesday, Wednesday…

17

SUNDAY

Have you ever come on anything quite like this extravagant generosity of God, this deep, deep wisdom?
It's way over our heads. We'll never figure it out.
Is there anyone around who can explain God?
Anyone smart enough to tell him what to do?
Anyone who has done him such a huge favor
that God has to ask his advice?

Everything comes from him;
  Everything happens through him;
  Everything ends up in him.
  Always glory! Always praise!
  Yes. Yes. Yes.
  Romans 11:33–36 MSG

To God belongs all the glory and the praise and the honor. Those who embrace that encounter a question—namely—
"How do I live in such a way as to give God His rightful praise?"
Once you experience the love of God, you naturally rouse a desire

to love in return. The response you return to Him can be identified with one word—*worship*. Our word *worship* is derived from an Old English word meaning to show honor.

The most used Hebrew word for *worship* in the Old Testament is *shachah*, and the most commonly used word in the New Testament is *proskunéō*. Both words mean to "bow down" or "crouch." Another Greek word for worship is defined as "to minister or serve."

Here in Part Three, I begin the "Days" series of chapters. Within these chapters, I will draw your attention to the ways in which you can worship—honor/serve—God. Unfortunately, due in great part to a gradual loss of understanding, many people have lost or never learned the great diversity of manners through which they can worship God. The natural results of such a loss prove plentiful. For example:

1. Some believers find worship boring.
2. Others think only of singing.
3. Still others think only of prayer.

These shortsighted views have, in addition, led to an over-complication and an isolation.

Over-complication = Worship must fit a certain format and, therefore, not everyone is capable.

Isolation = Worship is a "religious" exercise exclusively and, therefore, is limited to certain activities and occasions.

How can I put this? That's balderdash!

I will teach, over the span of this series of chapters, how you can worship God anywhere and anytime—and that you should.

Paul, Christ-follower, participated in and led communal worship; and he actively engaged in personal practices of worship. Inspired by God and fueled by personal experience, the apostle challenged Christians to worship God during all their days.

So here's what I want you to do, God helping you: Take your everyday, ordinary life—your sleeping, eating, going-to-work, and walking-around life—and place it before God as an offering.

Embracing what God does for you is the best thing you can do for him. Don't become so well-adjusted to your culture that you fit into it without even thinking. Instead, fix your attention on God. You'll be changed from the inside out. Readily recognize what he wants from you, and quickly respond to it.

Romans 12:1–2 MSG

These verses serve as our focal point for this section of the book. The *natural* response to God's love is to honor Him *every* day. Is it *yours*?

Honor Him with Sunday—

Soon after the resurrection of Jesus, believers (remembering that great Sunday event) started to meet for community worship on the first day of the week. We continue to do so today.

Since, borrowing the words of Klyne Snodgrass, Christianity is a "communal religion" and not a "me and Jesus" faith, you and I need and want to gather with other believers (174). We call such a gathering of believers a church. The Church universal is all believers—past, present, and future. The church local is a gathering of believers.

In Luke's gospel account, Peter accurately identifies Jesus as the Christ of God, the Messiah. Matthew's account of that same story includes another detail.

When Jesus arrived in the villages of Caesarea Philippi, he asked his disciples, "What are people saying about who the Son of Man is?"

They replied, "Some think he is John the Baptizer, some say Elijah, some Jeremiah or one of the other prophets."

He pressed them, "And how about you? Who do you say I am?"

Simon Peter said, "You're the Christ, the Messiah, the Son of the living God."

Matthew 16:13–16 MSG

That matches Luke. Then Matthew continues…

Jesus came back,

"God bless you, Simon, son of Jonah! You didn't get that answer out of books or from teachers. My Father in heaven, God himself, let you in on this secret of who I really am. And now I'm going to tell you who you are, really are. You are Peter, a rock. This is the rock on which I will put together my church, a church so expansive with energy that not even the gates of hell will be able to keep it out.

"And that's not all. You will have complete and free access to God's kingdom, keys to open any and every door: no more barriers between heaven and earth, earth and heaven. A yes on earth is yes in heaven. A no on earth is no in heaven."

Matthew 16:17–19 MSG

Jesus, who elsewhere promised to send the Spirit to guide, also promised to establish a body of believers—an *ekklēsia*, a church, an establishment that even hell itself cannot defeat. Hell can't beat it!

Sadly, however, hell doesn't even have to attempt to wage the war when so many believers throughout the history of the church have given up on her.

Gathering as the church fuels believers—strengthening our faith, courage, and commitment to each other. But that's not all.

Through followers of Jesus like yourselves gathered in churches, this extraordinary plan of God is becoming known and talked about even among the angels!

Ephesians 3:10 MSG

In 1919, Dr. William Riley wrote...

"We may say what we please against the local church, or against that larger body that we sometimes call 'the Church of God;' we may remind ourselves and our fellows that it is an imperfect institution; but the fact will forever remain that it is the medium of Christ's manifestation. God has received His glory in the Church by Jesus Christ; and it will forever remain a fact that God must receive His glory in the same institution, by the same glorious representative. The great secret hidden from the ages, was finally made known through the Church. It was to it that God voiced His power; through it that God declared His love; by it that God revealed His greatness..." (66).

Another wrote...

"The Church becomes a mirror through which the bright ones of heaven see the glory of God" (Wood 47).

Luke, in Acts, recounts how he and Paul arrived in Antioch and, upon coming to the church, they "saw the evidence of the grace of God." He adds, later, this word, "The disciples were called Christians first at Antioch."

I think it not a coincidence that the gathered believers were labeled Christians in the same location where the evidence of grace was displayed. C. S. Lewis wrote, "...the Church exists for nothing else but to draw men into Christ, to make them little Christs" (169).

The Antioch gathering was filled with Christians—with "little Christs." Little Christs display the evidence of the grace of God. What is the evidence?

- Love (John 13:35; Romans 12:9–21; 1 Corinthians 13)
- Service (Matthew 22:37–38; Galatians 5:13–14)
- Prayer(Matthew 21:12–13; 1 Thessalonians 5:16–18)

- Sound Doctrine (1 Timothy 1:1–11; 2 Timothy 3:16–4:5)
- Unity (John 17:20–26; Romans 15:5–7; Ephesians 4)
- The Fruit of the Spirit (Galatians 5:22–23)

It's good to look for and seek such things and live them out every day.

As you take your everyday ordinary life and lay it before God, start with Sunday.

18

MONDAY

On November 7, 2013, two Saudi Arabian league soccer teams faced off. The game looked like any other, that is, until a player experienced a shoelace problem. Something quite exceptional occurred. In the midst of competition, Jobson bent down and tied an opposing player's shoe and Leandro Bonfim missed a free kick—intentionally. Sports pages and social media wasted no time in spreading the word. Why? Because two soccer players chose to do the unexpected—they chose to help the other team. (Dowd)

Jesus said…

Luke 9:23—*Whoever wants to be my disciple must deny themselves and take up their cross daily and follow me.*

Within His words, particularly the final two, there is a challenge to seek an answer to the question, "How will I follow Jesus this year?"

That is a challenge well worth answering.

Chapters seventeen to twenty-three of this book aid you in that quest.

Following Jesus is a Sunday-through-Saturday pursuit. This

chapter focuses on Monday. We begin by revisiting the "Days" theme verses...

So here's what I want you to do, God helping you: Take your everyday, ordinary life—your sleeping, eating, going-to-work, and walking-around life—and place it before God as an offering. Embracing what God does for you is the best thing you can do for him. Don't become so well-adjusted to your culture that you fit into it without even thinking. Instead, fix your attention on God. You'll be changed from the inside out. Readily recognize what he wants from you, and quickly respond to it.

Romans 12:1–2 MSG

For better or for worse, the average person, particularly one dedicated to participating in church, does not consider Sunday to be an "everyday, ordinary" day. Most, however, certainly view Mondays as such.

Monday, the second day of the week, provides near countless opportunities during which you can glorify God. Whether *your* Monday is actually a Monday, you are given opportunities within your vocation to honor God with your actions. Whether an athlete, coach, lawyer, physician, student, parent, salesman, plumber, pastor, whatever —you, if you practice intentionality, discover how your work is more than a job.

It is a ministry opportunity. You discover, or already know, that your co-workers, employees, teachers, students, and children observe your actions—especially when you tie shoelaces in the middle of a game. Whoever said first, "Your actions speak louder than words," while perhaps devaluing the power of words, spoke apt words.

Recently I again read the Old Testament book, Ezra. The words of chapter seven, verse ten captured my mind and spoke to my heart.

Ezra had committed himself to studying the Revelation of God, to living it, and to teaching Israel to live its truths and ways.

Ezra 7:10 MSG

Ezra committed himself to three endeavors.

1. *Studying* the Revelation of God (the Bible).
2. *Living* it.
3. *Teaching.*

For this "Monday" chapter, I home in on his second endeavor —*Living it.* I lead our church staff in prayerfully designing each Sunday morning worship service and the weekly small groups to provide meaningful studying and teaching. Each participant adds power to those experiences through his or her personal times of Bible study. Those priceless endeavors serve as *means*, means to an end— namely, living our faith. Hear three strong voices on that fact.

Douglas Moo refers to Romans 12:1–2 as a "succinct description of the essence of the believer's *response* to God's grace" (394). Gerald Cragg, holding a like-minded view, suggested that, "The things we believe and the things we do fall apart with perilous ease.

Too often doctrine belongs to a theoretical world, remote from life and powerless to affect our daily conduct... Belief is sterile if it does not issue in a new quality of life" (578). Ernst Käsemann wrote, "Either the whole of Christian life is worship and the gatherings and sacramental acts of the community provide equipment and instruction for this, or these gatherings and acts lead in fact to absurdity" (qtd in Moo, 754).

When others see your life, do they see your response to God's grace as sterile and absurd or as thriving and fruitful?

It is fitting as we focus on Monday, the day (literally or metaphorically) when people watch to see how they are *living* their faith, that I highlight the ground floor, or foundation, of evangelism. Evangelism begins with living one's faith, not *to be* seen, but *as you are* seen. Those who seek meaning in life will listen to a Christian tell of the love of Jesus if he or she lives the love of Jesus.

I designed a test to serve as a tool for use in evaluating the degree to which one lives the love of God on Mondays—*"everyday ordinary life."* Score yourself and don't worry about others grading you.

"Living It" Test

Make it your ambition to lead a quiet life: You should mind your own business and work with your hands, just as we told you, so that your daily life may win the respect of outsiders...
1 Thessalonians 4:11–12a

Grade (A, B, C, D, F)

____ Patience with my _____ (teacher, co-workers, spouse, children, etc.)

____ Doing *all things* as if for the Lord (Colossians 3:17, 23)

____ Respecting my _____ (teacher, co-workers, boss, parents, etc.)

____ Taming my tongue (Ephesians 4:29; James 3:1–12)

____ Caring for others (Matthew 22:39; Philippians 2:4)

____ Rejecting selfishness (Mark 10:35–45; Philippians 2:4)

____ Controlling anger (Proverbs 29:11; Galatians 5:16–26)

Eric Liddell, the great British athlete, whose story is depicted in the movie *Chariots of Fire*, sought to honor God in all he did, whether on the track or on the mission field. A challenge he offered greatly helps the preparation for Monday. "Have a great aim—have a high standard —make Jesus your ideal...make him an ideal not merely to be admired but also to be followed."

19

TUESDAY

Fifty-five.

That number represents the approximate number of hours annually a person will devote to gathering in church for worship. That assumes attendance each Sunday morning of the year plus special services.

The remaining 8,705 hours of the year are devoted to various other activities.

In chapter seventeen, devoted to learning from God's Word about the importance of worshiping together at church, I emphasized the divine call to gather to praise and glorify His name. While doing so, I directed your attention to an even more encompassing charge.

So here's what I want you to do, God helping you: Take your everyday, ordinary life—your sleeping, eating, going-to-work, and walking-around life—and place it before God as an offering. Embracing what God does for you is the best thing you can do for him. Don't become so well-adjusted to your culture that you fit into it without even thinking. Instead, fix your attention on God. You'll be changed from the inside out. Readily recognize what he wants from you, and quickly respond to it.

Romans 12:1–2 MSG

In line with such a charge, in the last chapter, I addressed the vital importance of giving your vocation to God as an offering or, in other words, to take God with you as you work. If you took that to heart and responded to that invitation, then you are in the process of devoting some 2,100 to 2,500 hours to Him.

So, assuming that my math is correct, if you devote 55 hours to worship and around 2,300 hours to work, you still have 6,405 hours with which to honor God. Therefore, in this chapter, I want to draw your attention to Tuesdays.

Why Tuesdays? Well Tuesdays are the days on which the teenage students and children of our church gather for small group time. Our adults participate in small groups either on Tuesdays or another day. So for consistency's sake, I chose Tuesday as the appropriate title for this chapter.

Return to the number fifty-five.

Here's a question. Can anyone sustain a thriving relationship with the Creator and Savior on fifty-five hours a year? No! We need (Need!) more time of focused worship, study, and time with other believers.

Read God's words on the matter.

1) Psalm 122:1

I rejoiced with those who said to me, "Let us go to the house of the Lord."

2) 1 Corinthians 12:12–27

Just as a body, though one, has many parts, but all its many parts form one body, so it is with Christ. For we were all baptized by one Spirit so as to form one body—whether Jews or Gentiles, slave or free —and we were all given the one Spirit to drink. Even so the body is not made up of one part but of many.

Now if the foot should say, "Because I am not a hand, I do not belong to the body," it would not for that reason stop being part of the body. And if the ear should say, "Because I am not an eye, I do not belong to the body," it would not for that reason stop being part of the body. If the whole body were an eye, where would the sense of hearing be? If the whole body were an ear, where would the sense of smell be? But in fact God has placed the parts in the body, every one of them, just as he wanted them to be. If they were all one part, where would the body be? As it is, there are many parts, but one body.

The eye cannot say to the hand, "I don't need you!" And the head cannot say to the feet, "I don't need you!" On the contrary, those parts of the body that seem to be weaker are indispensable, and the parts that we think are less honorable we treat with special honor. And the parts that are unpresentable are treated with special modesty, while our presentable parts need no special treatment. But God has put the body together, giving greater honor to the parts that lacked it, so that there should be no division in the body, but that its parts should have equal concern for each other. If one part suffers, every part suffers with it; if one part is honored, every part rejoices with it.

Now you are the body of Christ, and each one of you is a part of it.

3) Hebrews 3:13–14

But encourage one another daily, as long as it is called "Today," so that none of you may be hardened by sin's deceitfulness. We have come to share in Christ, if indeed we hold our original conviction firmly to the very end.

4) Hebrews 10:25

And let us not neglect our meeting together, as some people do, but encourage one another, especially now that the day of his return is drawing near.

Every Christ follower needs to participate in a community of Christian faith. That community needs to be both in the larger setting (those fifty-five hours) as well as times in a smaller setting. Look to the example of the first believers.

They devoted themselves to the apostles' teaching and to fellowship, to the breaking of bread and to prayer. Everyone was filled with awe at the many wonders and signs performed by the apostles. All the believers were together and had everything in common. They sold property and possessions to give to anyone who had need. Every day they continued to meet together in the temple courts. They broke bread in their homes and ate together with glad and sincere hearts, praising God and enjoying the favor of all the people. And the Lord added to their number daily those who were being saved.

Acts 2:42–47

Within this text, rich examples and truths emerge. While the words recording the historical events are not a dictate to sell everything and adjust to communal living, there is within them a strong call to mirror the early followers' actions as to generosity and community.

In regard to that latter word, *community*, it must be used with intentionality. The Greek word for such a community or fellowship is *koinōnia. Koinōnia* is a fellowship tied together as a bond.

Dr. Frank Stagg, the late Baptist pastor and theologian, wrote a helpful word…

"[E]arly Christians were not a mere society of co-operating people but a community in the deepest sense. Macmurray has demonstrated the important fact of an essential difference between two types of association: 'There is a type of association which is constituted by a common purpose. There is another which consists in sharing a common life'" (67–68).

He continues by expanding on Macmurray's distinguishing between "society" and "community." Suggesting, correctly, that even gang members have society, even a common goal; but they do not have true community. Community requires devotion, shared purpose, and humility. German theologian Karl Barth wrote, "Genuine fellowship is grounded upon a negative: it is grounded upon what men lack. Precisely when we recognize that we are sinners do we perceive that we are brothers" (qtd in Stagg 70).

In church community, sinners come together as brothers and sisters. Theodore Ferris wrote, "The church should be the center of a community life in which the lonely find friends, the sinful find understanding and forgiveness, the believers find the support of those who believe the same things" (52).

Support, understanding, and community occur most fruitfully in smaller settings. Here are some practical applications for such settings. I refer to them as life groups.

Experiencing Community in Life Groups through...

1. Study (vs 42a—"They devoted themselves to the apostles' teaching.")
2. Shared Food
a. Meals
b. Communion
3. Prayer
4. Sincerity
5. Praise

Now notice the result.

Acts 2:47b—*And the Lord added to their number daily those who were being saved.*

As Christ-followers engage in worship together, they grow in unity, strength, and number. This growth leads to continually reaching more and more for Christ and teaching them as they grow in Him. As people connect in small groups, they are not (unless they choose to be) lost in the crowd.

While I am not suggesting that it will or should "stick," for today, let the slogan of this chapter be..."Fifty-five is not enough!"

20

WEDNESDAY

In our pursuit of knowledge as to how to live in such a manner that we honor God each of the seven days of each week, we continue with Wednesday.

So here's what I want you to do, God helping you: Take your everyday, ordinary life—your sleeping, eating, going-to-work, and walking-around life—and place it before God as an offering.

Romans 12:1 MSG

As we continue to focus on that call, let me recap.
Sunday = Honor God through worship.
Monday = Honor God with your work.
Tuesday = Honor God by dedicating more than fifty-five hours a year to Him.
With three days before and three days after Wednesday, the day earns the title "Hump Day"—as masterfully portrayed by the camel in the Geico commercial. Wednesday represents all of those desperate pleas that begin with the words, "If I can just…"—words followed with an assortment of…

- "get through"
- "catch up"
- "make it to tomorrow"

and statements like those.

Wednesday marks the day on which people grow weary.

While not necessarily on Wednesday, everyone grows weary. In Isaiah 40, the prophet declares, "even youths grow tired and weary."

Knowing our need for rest, Jesus extended an invitation to all to come to Him to find such a seemingly elusive gift. Continuing with the theme, the apostle Paul encouraged his hearers to not become weary doing good.

Weariness invades everyone's life; it is no respecter of persons. Toddlers learning to walk, children up too late, teenagers cramming for exams, moms and dads tending to children at three a.m., young professionals burning the midnight oil, senior adults worn down by the years—all know weariness. Does a solution exist? Can we prevail?

The answers to those questions return us to familiar territory—to the arena of "easier said than done." Yet, nevertheless, the affirmative "yes" answers both questions. So—what's the solution? How can you prevail?

Before I show you in Scripture, the *what* and *how*, respectively—a reminder of our essence will prove helpful. The Word of God drives home the amazing truth that God created you. You did not arrive due to some accidental progression of nature. You were created and in God's image you were created.

When He formed you, He gifted you with a body, a soul, and a spirit. While the discussions prove complex, in summary, we exist as physical, emotional, and spiritual beings. Therefore, in regard to the subject at hand, we grow weary physically, emotionally, and spiritually.

With that grounding, we return now to the questions—

"What's the solution?" and "How can we prevail?"

One answer belongs to both.

REST

That's it! The cure for weariness is, in a word—rest.

Saying does not equal doing, so let's unpack some ways to accomplish this. In this chapter, in recognition of "Wednesday," I will provide some starter tools from Scripture to help you get over the hump. (You can also refer back to chapter eleven for a refresher.) Keep in mind—rest is not reserved for one day alone.

Tools for *Physical* Rest—

1. *Trust* in the Lord.
2. *Sleep* in trust.

Unless the Lord builds the house, the builders labor in vain. Unless the Lord watches over the city, the guards stand watch in vain. In vain you rise early and stay up late, toiling for food to eat—for he grants sleep to those he loves.

Psalm 127:1–2

Tools for *Emotional* Rest—

The longtime Alaskan Ella Bell lived to the age of 101. When she celebrated her hundredth birthday, she was asked to share her secret to longevity…

"Don't worry. I give all my worries to God. The world could be falling apart and I wouldn't worry. I'd just bake an apple pie." (Alaska Centenarians)

We may safely assume that Ella Bell learned her pie recipe from her mother and that she learned to give up worry from her Lord.

Therefore I tell you, do not worry about your life, what you will eat or drink; or about your body, what you will wear. Is not life more than food, and the body more than clothes? Look at the birds of the air; they do not sow or reap or store away in barns, and yet your heavenly Father feeds them. Are you not much more valuable than they? Can any one of you by worrying add a single hour to your life?

"And why do you worry about clothes? See how the flowers of the field grow. They do not labor or spin. Yet I tell you that not even Solomon in all his splendor was dressed like one of these. If that is how God clothes the grass of the field, which is here today and tomorrow is thrown into the fire, will he not much more clothe you— you of little faith? So do not worry, saying, 'What shall we eat?' or 'What shall we drink?' or 'What shall we wear?' For the pagans run after all these things, and your heavenly Father knows that you need them. But seek first his kingdom and his righteousness, and all these things will be given to you as well. Therefore do not worry about tomorrow, for tomorrow will worry about itself. Each day has enough trouble of its own.

Matthew 6:25–34

1. *Trust* in the Lord.
2. *Kick* your *worry habit*.
3. *Find* a friend. (Listening ear, encourager, small group member, a fellow retiree, another young mom, another new dad, a peer at your school who follows Jesus, etc.)

Tools for *Spiritual* Rest—

1. *Trust* in the Lord.
2. *Look* upward.

I lift up my eyes to the mountains—where does my help come from? My help comes from the Lord, the Maker of heaven and earth.

Psalm 121:1–2

John Wesley once wrote to a friend, "You look *in*ward too much, and *up*ward too little" (Source Unknown).

3. *Look* outward.

Therefore if you have any encouragement from being united with Christ, if any comfort from his love, if any common sharing in the Spirit, if any tenderness and compassion, then make my joy complete by being like-minded, having the same love, being one in spirit and of one mind. Do nothing out of selfish ambition or vain conceit. Rather, in humility value others above yourselves, not looking to your own interests but each of you to the interests of the others.

Philippians 2:1–4

Notice that while mentioning *up*ward and *out*ward, I did not include *in*ward. A quick Google search will produce for you a near-endless list of resources that offer advice on how to find peace and rest. If you choose that route, you will find some helpful tools. However, you will also find much more "in" than "up" and "out."

A life focused on self will not produce the rest that God offers. True rest arrives when we devote ourselves to loving God and loving others. Selfishness leads to spiritual fatigue. Service leads to rest that accompanies obedience to God's greatest commandment. Live for Him and others and you will find rest.

While I highly recommend Sunday naps, one day to sleep in, and a trip to Hawaii during Alaskan winters, I also offer a word of wisdom—not mine—God's…

Come to me, all you who are weary and burdened, and I will give you rest. Take my yoke upon you and learn from me, for I am gentle and humble in heart, and you will find rest for your souls. For my yoke is easy and my burden is light.

Matthew 11:28–30

Thomas á Kempis wrote, in the early 1400s, the now-classic Christian devotional book *The Imitation of Christ*. In it, he composed a prayer—a prayer with which I will close this chapter and in which I invite you to join me in praying.

"My Lord Jesus, I beseech you, do not be far from me, but come quickly and help me, for vain thoughts have risen in my heart and worldly fears have troubled me sorely. How shall I break them down? How shall I go unhurt without your help?

I shall go before you, says our Lord; I shall drive away the pride of your heart; then shall I set open to you the gates of spiritual knowledge and show you the privacy of my secrets.

O Lord, do as you say, and then all wicked imaginings shall flee away from me. Truly, this is my hope and my only comfort—to fly to you in every trouble, to trust steadfastly in you, to call inwardly upon you, and to abide patiently your coming and your heavenly consolations which, I trust, will quickly come to me" (qtd in Job 256).

21

THURSDAY

For what do you wait? A restaurant's name sheds light on the epidemic called waiting. Whether literally thanking God or not, masses of people celebrate the arrival of Friday. Acknowledging that fact, I urge restraint from longing so for Fridays that valuable Thursday is passed up.

During this fifth of seven chapters in the "Days" chapters, I aim to uphold the value of Thursdays—not necessarily the fifth day of the week, yet the Thursdays (also known as periods of waiting) or as a pastor friend (Rev. Leon May) deems them, "the meantimes."

For what do *you* wait?

You and I engage in periods of waiting for exciting things—such as the fish to bite, weddings, births, birthdays, reunions, graduations, restorations, etc.

You and I also experience periods of waiting for remedies to negative things—such as arguments, illnesses, loss of employment, insurance settlements, custody battles, etc.

If, as I hope and encourage, you continue to answer the question, "How will I follow Jesus this year?"—you must include within your answer a word on how you engage in waiting.

How well do you wait?

Two passages from God's word offer perfect words of wisdom for those setting out to give Thursdays to God. The first of the two passages is in Romans.

> *So here's what I want you to do, God helping you: Take your everyday, ordinary life—your sleeping, eating, going-to-work, and walking-around life—and place it before God as an offering.*

Romans 12:1 MSG

As we have done throughout these chapters, we listen to Paul's charge to the Roman Christians and then recognize that through the words, God speaks to twenty-first-century Christians just as boldly and clearly.

Each and every Thursday in life (literally and figuratively) belongs in the "everyday, ordinary life" category. No exceptions. Therefore, take your waiting and "place it before God as an offering."

When you do, unless you are exceptionally unique, you will face frustration. That proves the rule, rather than the exception.

Around the year 1010 BC, a young man named David answered God's call to reign as Israel's second king. During his forty-year reign, David, while certainly no saint himself, experienced the death of two children, betrayal by friend and family, assassination attempts, coups, a mocking spouse, near-constant foreign invasion, and much more of the like. Israel's king, one known as the man after God's own heart, did not hesitate to have a few "heart-to-hearts" with his Creator. We find one such emotionally charged cry in Psalm 13 (our second passage for this chapter).

> *How long, Lord? Will you forget me forever?*
> *How long will you hide your face from me?*
> *How long must I wrestle with my thoughts*
> *and day after day have sorrow in my heart?*
> *How long will my enemy triumph over me?*
> *Look on me and answer, Lord my God.*
> *Give light to my eyes, or I will sleep in death,*

and my enemy will say, "I have overcome him,"
and my foes will rejoice when I fall.

Psalm 13:1–4

I expect some God-fearing soul to rise up now and say the religious form of "Don't you talk to my mama like that!"

Do we dare question God?

David did.

Do we dare demand His hearing?

David did.

How dare we?

J.R.P. Sclater's words of a century ago resonate. He wrote. "The outcry of heaviness is evidently in order, provided that the man who makes it is still a seeker" (73).

Echoing Sclater several years later, Gerald Wilson argues that...

"This need not be silent suffering...The experience of divine abandonment is real and painful and is rightfully brought to God in laments and questions. God is not offended by our honest questions or even our heated complaints. Both confirm our desire for relationship and our faith that all is not as it should be" (284).

Take note of that which David accuses God...

Verse 1 — Forgetting

Verse 1 — Hiding

Theologically, believers know that God does not forget (except in a voluntary keeping-our-sins-not-against-us) and that He dwells with His people and remains faithful, rather than hiding behind corners or excuses.

Experientially, however, believers feel that God does forget or, at least, chooses to ignore and that He disappears and even holds grudges. And so often, the experiential clouds over the theological.

With Philistines, Amalekites, and an egomaniacal predecessor running amuck around him, David's theology grew weak in the knees.

In your periods of waiting, who or what runs amuck? Whose actions or what situations stretch your faith plastic-wrap thin?

In those times, whether moments or (seemingly) lifetimes, heed the four-centuries-old words of advice from Bishop Thomas Ken,

"Stand but your ground, your ghostly foes will fly—

Hell trembles at a heaven-directed eye" (qtd in Spurgeon. Vol. 1, part 2, 18).

Read that sentence again—the *entire* sentence. Attempting to stand your ground without an eye toward heaven is foolhardy, at best. Yes, stupid, actually; dare I say?

David chose wisely as he stood his ground. We hear of such in the conclusion of his psalm. Return there.

> *But I trust in your unfailing love;*
> *my heart rejoices in your salvation.*
> *I will sing the Lord's praise,*
> *for he has been good to me.*
> *Psalm 13:5–6*

"But"—I really like the tune-changing power of that word!

Because David chose to keep an eye heaven-directed, he could *trust, rejoice,* and *sing* even. A question arises with this heaven-gazing image. For what does one look? David, thankfully, does not make his readers guess. He looks to at least two things.

Psalm 13:5—*But I trust in your unfailing love; my heart rejoices in your salvation.*

First, he returns to his theology—to the truth. He focuses specifically upon two theological truths.

1. God's unfailing love.
2. God's salvation.

Good theology is a must for faith. Don't neglect the Word! Theology fuels faith. As one scholar wrote, "Faith has its own logic" (Taylor 74).

Second, in order to wait in a healthy manner, David looks to his memories. David remembers.

Psalm 13:6b—*for he has been good to me.*

Charles Spurgeon heralded that "Hope is heaven's balm for present sorrow" (Vol. 1, part 2, 5).

Hindsight strengthens hope. For sure, not all memories prove pleasant; some are downright painful. Therefore, one must look back through the lens of faith. Look intently and you will see the hand of God either protecting you or lifting you out of the pit of pain. David, in reflection, couldn't bring life to his deceased sons or undo his own follies; but he did see God's power in providing comfort and forgiveness. As you wait, look back and remember God's goodness.

Needtobreathe, one of my favorite bands, sings the song, "Keep Your Eyes Open." Hear a few of the lyrics.

"Keep your eyes… Open, my love

So show me your fire, show me your heart

You know I'll never let you fall apart

If you keep your eyes… Open"

A more familiar tune's lyrics ring out from even the youngest tongues…

"God is so good.

God is so good.

God is so good.

He's so good to me!"

Do you believe that?

Do you believe that during times of difficulty? We know from experience that hardship is a reality of life and especially so during periods of waiting, in "the meantimes." Perhaps you are familiar with the sociological term, *communitas.*

Communitas—the sense of sharing and intimacy that develops among persons who experience liminality as a group.

Within the definition there is another not-commonly used word— namely, *liminality.* "In anthropology, *liminality* (from the Latin word *līmen*, meaning "a threshold" is the term used in reference to in-the-meantimes—those times when we wait. Times when those who are experiencing disorientation and questioning are being formed into what they *will* be. One source explains, "During a…liminal stage, participants 'stand at the threshold' between their previous way of structuring their identity, time, or community, and a new way..." (Wikipedia).

Each person in his or her own way waits for communitas; let us wait *together*. In the words of the apostle Paul...

If one part suffers, every part suffers with it; if one part is honored, every part rejoices with it. 1 Corinthians 12:26

During the Thursdays of your life, trust in God's unfailing love and rely on each other for strength to prevail.

Return to David. This time he sits patiently before God. Questions remain. Doubts creep in. Yet there he sits, speaking to his Creator with words no longer laced with rage. Then he records his words—composing lyrics of praise. While David yelled out Psalm 13 while the pain was fresh and his thoughts were clouded, he now breathes calmly, perhaps with tears on his cheeks, and sings Psalm 27.

> *The Lord is my light and my salvation—*
> *whom shall I fear?*
> *The Lord is the stronghold of my life—*
> *of whom shall I be afraid?*
> *When the wicked advance against me*
> *to devour me,*
> *it is my enemies and my foes*
> *who will stumble and fall.*
> *Though an army besiege me,*
> *my heart will not fear;*
> *though war break out against me,*
> *even then I will be confident.*
> *One thing I ask from the Lord,*
> *this only do I seek:*
> *that I may dwell in the house of the Lord*
> *all the days of my life,*
> *to gaze on the beauty of the Lord*
> *and to seek him in his temple.*
> *For in the day of trouble*

he will keep me safe in his dwelling;
he will hide me in the shelter of his sacred tent
and set me high upon a rock.
Then my head will be exalted
above the enemies who surround me;
at his sacred tent I will sacrifice with shouts of joy;
I will sing and make music to the Lord.
Hear my voice when I call, Lord;
be merciful to me and answer me.
My heart says of you, "Seek his face!"
Your face, Lord, I will seek.
Do not hide your face from me,
do not turn your servant away in anger;
you have been my helper.
Do not reject me or forsake me,
God my Savior.
Though my father and mother forsake me,
the Lord will receive me.
Teach me your way, Lord;
lead me in a straight path
because of my oppressors.
Do not turn me over to the desire of my foes,
for false witnesses rise up against me,
spouting malicious accusations.
I remain confident of this:
I will see the goodness of the Lord
in the land of the living.
Wait for the Lord;
be strong and take heart
and wait for the Lord.

Psalm 27

22

FRIDAY

Welcome to Friday! So far in the "Days" chapters, I have connected five days of the week with a corresponding act of honoring God.

- Sunday = Honor God through *worship*.
- Monday = Honor God with your *work*.
- Tuesday = Honor God with *more than fifty-five*.
- Wednesday = Honor God by *resting*.
- Thursday = Honor God while *waiting*.

God calls us to honor Him with the first five days of the week along with the last two.

So here's what I want you to do, God helping you: Take your everyday, ordinary life—your sleeping, eating, going-to-work, and walking-around life—and place it before God as an offering. Embracing what God does for you is the best thing you can do for him. Don't become so well-adjusted to your culture that you fit into it without even thinking. Instead, fix your attention on God. You'll be changed from the inside out. Readily recognize what he wants from you, and quickly respond to it. Romans 12:1–2 MSG

In this chapter, join me, won't you, in exploring how you can "take your everyday, ordinary" Friday and place it before God as an offering. I use the sixth day of the week as the day that represents Pay Day. Four chapters ago, I taught how to honor God with your work; now I turn to teaching on how to honor God with what you earn for your work—your money.

Experts tell you and me to refrain from speaking about religion and politics in "polite" company. Some will also tell you and me to refrain from speaking about sex and money in church. Well, with the exception of politics, I ignore their advice.

In this chapter—writing rather than speaking and continuing to ignore—I will "talk" about money. When I do, I join the likes of King David, the Lord Jesus, the apostle Peter, James the brother of Jesus, and John the disciple.

Why do so many references to money and possessions occur in the Scriptures? Because, as the saying goes, "the two great tests of character are wealth and poverty," and because of the fact that of all the various competitors for admiration and attention, Jesus spoke of one most.

Matthew 6:24—*No one can serve two masters. Either you will hate the one and love the other, or you will be devoted to the one and despise the other. You cannot serve both God and money.*

In light of the Lord's words, Rick Warren writes…

"[Jesus] didn't say, 'You *should not,*' but 'You *cannot.*' It is impossible. Living for ministry and living for money are mutually exclusive goals. Which one will you choose? If you're a servant of God, you can't moonlight for yourself. *All* your time belongs to God. He insists on exclusive allegiance, not part-time faithfulness.

Money has the greatest potential to replace God in your life. More people are sidetracked from serving by materialism than by anything else. They say, 'After I achieve my financial goals, I'm going to serve God.' That is a foolish decision they will regret for eternity. When Jesus is your Master, money serves you, but if money is your master, you become its slave. Wealth is certainly not a sin, but failing to use it for God's glory is. Servants of God are always more concerned about ministry than money.

The Bible is very clear: God uses money to test your faithfulness as a servant. That is why Jesus talked more about money than he did about either heaven or hell. He said, *'If you have not been trustworthy in handling worldly wealth, who will trust you with true riches?'* How you manage your money affects how much God can bless your life" (267).

I dare say that most who read this chapter will agree that we choose best when we choose God; yet, we will at the same time acknowledge the very real struggle that we face with refusing to allow the thoughts of and quest for money to enter our minds and pull on our strength.

Several years after Jesus spoke those words in Matthew, He blinded a man on a road. The blindness opened the man's eyes to the truth. Paul, that man, confessed at a later date that he knew what it was to possess much and to lack much, yet he learned a secret. Do you want to know his secret?

Catch this! His secret was being content. (Remember "Top Ten"— #10?) Followers of Jesus honor God with their Fridays and, in order to do so, learn the secret of being content. Paul expounded on contentment in his first letter to the young man Timothy.

But godliness with contentment is great gain. For we brought nothing into the world, and we can take nothing out of it. But if we have food and clothing, we will be content with that. Those who want to get rich fall into temptation and a trap and into many foolish and harmful desires that plunge people into ruin and destruction. For the love of money is a root of all kinds of evil. Some people, eager for money, have wandered from the faith and pierced themselves with many griefs.

But you, man of God, flee from all this, and pursue righteousness, godliness, faith, love, endurance and gentleness. Fight the good fight of the faith. Take hold of the eternal life to which you were called when you made your good confession in the presence of many witnesses. In the sight of God, who gives life to everything, and of Christ Jesus, who while testifying before Pontius Pilate made the good confession, I charge you to keep this command without spot or blame until the appearing of our Lord Jesus Christ, which God will bring about in his own time—God, the blessed and only Ruler, the King of kings and Lord of lords, who alone is immortal and who lives in unapproachable light, whom no one has seen or can see. To him be honor and might forever. Amen.

Command those who are rich in this present world not to be arrogant nor to put their hope in wealth, which is so uncertain, but to put their hope in God, who richly provides us with everything for our enjoyment. Command them to do good, to be rich in good deeds, and to be generous and willing to share. In this way they will lay up treasure for themselves as a firm foundation for the coming age, so that they may take hold of the life that is truly life.

Timothy, guard what has been entrusted to your care. Turn away from godless chatter and the opposing ideas of what is falsely called knowledge, which some have professed and in so doing have departed from the faith.

Grace be with you all.

1 Timothy 6:6–21

These verses provide such great insight for the quest to honor God with money as well as character traits to which every man and woman who longs to honor God should commit.

Commit to:

1. *Humility*

Verse 6—*But godliness with contentment is great gain.*

Phillip Keller wrote…

"Contentment should be the hallmark of the man or woman who has just put his or her affairs in the hands of God" (17–18).

Contentment strengthens humility. Humility is not optional for the follower of Jesus.

King David wrote countless songs, several of which we hear in Psalms. Here are the lyrics with which he begins three of those.

Psalm 23:1—*The Lord is my shepherd, I lack nothing*

Psalm 24:1—*The earth is the Lord's, and everything in it, the world, and all who live in it*

Psalm 25:1–2a—*In you, Lord my God, I put my trust. I trust in you; do not let me be put to shame.*

Pride says, "This is *my* money and I will do with it as *I* please."

Humility says, "This is *God's* money and I will do with it as *He* pleases."

Verse 17a—*Command those who are rich in this present world not to be arrogant.*

2. *Integrity*

Verses 9–10:

Those who want to get rich fall into temptation and a trap and into many foolish and harmful desires that plunge people into ruin and destruction. For the love of money is a root of all kinds of evil. Some people, eager for money, have wandered from the faith and pierced themselves with many griefs.

"Temptation," "trap," "love," "eager for"—that sounds like a love affair. Just as in a marriage, integrity means faithfulness. Solomon shared priceless words with regard to integrity.

Proverbs 11:3—*The integrity of the upright guides them, but the unfaithful are destroyed by their duplicity.*

Practice integrity by:

Paying your taxes; paying your debts; let your financial yes be yes and your financial no be no; pay your employees well; do not steal.

. . .

3. *Generosity*

Verses 17–18:

Command those who are rich in this present world not to be arrogant nor to put their hope in wealth, which is so uncertain, but to put their hope in God, who richly provides us with everything for our enjoyment. Command them to do good, to be rich in good deeds, and to be generous and willing to share.

Solomon agrees…

One person gives freely, yet gains even more;
another withholds unduly, but comes to poverty.
A generous person will prosper;
whoever refreshes others will be refreshed. Proverbs 11:24–25

God's people, following His example, should be the most generous people on the planet. John, in his letter, tells us that, *We love because [God] first loved us.* Borrow that and may it be said of us that "we give because He first gave to us."

Generosity breeds generosity.

Practice generosity by:

Give your tithes; give your offerings; meet the needs of others; *look not only to your own interests, but also to the interests of others.*

Once you commit to these three traits, you lay the foundation for a lasting benefit.

4. *Perpetuity*

Solomon, one of the wealthiest men in all of history, made an interesting observation when he wrote…

Proverbs 11:4—*Wealth is worthless in the day of wrath, but righteousness delivers from death.*

Paul agreed. In his writing to Timothy, he highlighted the end result of humility, integrity, and generosity.

1 Timothy 6:19—*In this way they will lay up treasure for themselves as a firm foundation for the coming age, so that they may take hold of the life that is truly life.*

Humility, integrity, and generosity last into perpetuity. Let us not forget the truth found back in verse 7.

Verse 7—*For we brought nothing into the world, and we can take nothing out of it.*

These traits are awfully difficult to pursue. However, much more remains. God calls His followers to practice healthy money management for reasons that might surprise you. Return to verse 17.

*God...richly provides us with everything **for our enjoyment.*** (Emphasis mine.)

The Greek word from which we translate *enjoyment* is *apŏlausis.* That word expresses the idea of full enjoyment.

As with any gift from God—sleep, food, sex—money can be greatly enjoyed when used according to His will. God is not a killjoy. He provides as the loving Father who finds pleasure in blessing His children. Enjoy what God has given you in a way that honors Him.

As John the disciple wrote to one of the seven churches in Revelation, he recorded an indictment in regard to money.

Revelation 3:17—*You say, "I am rich; I have acquired wealth and do not need a thing." But you do not realize that you are wretched, pitiful, poor, blind and naked.*

How can a man be *pitiful, poor, blind, and naked* even as he is rich? How can a woman *gain the whole world, yet lose [her] own soul*?

By giving in to temptation by embracing *pride, falsehood,* and *greed* rather than *humility, integrity,* and *generosity.*

23

SATURDAY

Teresa of Avila, a Christian from the sixteenth century, prayed, even as one who at the young age of fourteen lost her mother to death, for God to deliver her from "gloomy people" and "frowning saints" (Gossip 491).

One would rightly surmise that among the forgiven, the people of faith, would be found the most joyous people on the planet earth. Thankfully, the same one could move beyond inferring to observing joyous followers of Christ. "Redeemed How I Love to Proclaim It," "Shout to the Lord," and "We Will Not Be Shaken" they sing.

Sadly, however, the same one could observe believers whose demeanor reflects an appearance fitting of a funeral dirge.

If those somber souls do indeed possess some happiness, their hearts, as of yet, have not told their faces. You see, some get stuck on "wretch like me" and fail ever to claim the "Amazing Grace." Lauren Daigle, in her song "How Can It Be," thankfully, moves from…

"I've been hiding, afraid I've let You down.

Inside I doubt that You still love me."

To…

"But in Your eyes there's only grace now."

Grace—the undeserved free gift from your Creator.

Grace—now that should make you happy.

To start off His most well-known sermon, Jesus chose an impactful and surprising first word: μακάριοι. Most Bible translations record that Greek word with the English *blessed*. While appropriate, that word often hinders our hearing. The word *blessed* rarely brings to mind more than some sort of religious terminology. A better understanding of Jesus' choice of word is grasped when one learns that the word μακάριοι means *happy*. He repeats the word eight times during His introduction and then He declares…

Matthew 5:12—*Rejoice and be glad, because great is your reward in heaven, for in the same way they persecuted the prophets who were before you.*

Rejoice and be glad!

In a somewhat less well-known teaching occasion, one in His own hometown, Jesus opened the Hebrew Scriptures and read.

He went to Nazareth, where he had been brought up, and on the Sabbath day he went into the synagogue, as was his custom. He stood up to read, and the scroll of the prophet Isaiah was handed to him. Unrolling it, he found the place where it is written:

"The Spirit of the Lord is on me,
　　because he has anointed me
　　to proclaim good news to the poor.
He has sent me to proclaim freedom for the prisoners
　　and recovery of sight for the blind,
　　to set the oppressed free,
　　to proclaim the year of the Lord's favor."

Then he rolled up the scroll, gave it back to the attendant and sat down. The eyes of everyone in the synagogue were fastened on him. He began by saying to them, "Today this scripture is fulfilled in your hearing."

Luke 4:16–21

Good news. Freedom. Recovery. Release. Lord's favor.

See His smile? Hear His joy?

Jesus taught and shared His personal joy. He invited others to join Him in it. One such day occurs when a man and a woman stand before God and witnesses to wed. While they often prove stressful to plan, during the ceremony as the groom half hears the preacher due to the beauty of his bride and the bride prepares for that delightful kiss, weddings inspire joy. It is in such setting that we find Jesus.

On the third day a wedding took place at Cana in Galilee. Jesus' mother was there, and Jesus and his disciples had also been invited to the wedding. When the wine was gone, Jesus' mother said to him, "They have no more wine."

"Woman, why do you involve me?" Jesus replied. "My hour has not yet come."

His mother said to the servants, "Do whatever he tells you."

Nearby stood six stone water jars, the kind used by the Jews for ceremonial washing, each holding from twenty to thirty gallons.

Jesus said to the servants, "Fill the jars with water"; so they filled them to the brim.

Then he told them, "Now draw some out and take it to the master of the banquet."

They did so, and the master of the banquet tasted the water that had been turned into wine. He did not realize where it had come from, though the servants who had drawn the water knew. Then he called the bridegroom aside and said, "Everyone brings out the choice wine first and then the cheaper wine after the guests have had too much to drink; but you have saved the best till now."

What Jesus did here in Cana of Galilee was the first of the signs through which he revealed his glory; and his disciples believed in him.

John 2:1–11

I understand with no difficulty why Jesus would restore sight to the blind and cause once-useless legs to run. I, however, scratch my head here a bit. What eternal difference does replenished wine make? Shouldn't He have been preaching somewhere or at least feeding the hungry who had no food rather than restocking the reception line? Yet then I reread the wisdom of Mary.

John 2:5—*His mother said to the servants, "Do whatever he tells you."*

When we looked at this passage from the perspective of #5 in Jesus' Top Ten, it was to

recognize that Jesus honored Mary. Jesus knows what He's doing. He did nothing without

purpose. In His wisdom, He addressed the moment of crisis at the celebration.

Why the wine?

In one word—joy. He turned water into wine to extend the joy of that grand occasion. Jesus inspired the authors of Scripture, including Paul's command *Do not get drunk on wine,* so we know He was not, in His first miracle, blessing public intoxication. He was, however, blessing the newlyweds with a refreshment that added to the joyous celebration.

The religiously pious falsely accused the Lord of gluttony and drunkenness. They did so in part, I believe, because they had lost their joy.

I greatly enjoy hearing David's plea in Psalm 51.

Psalm 51:12a—*Restore to me the joy of your salvation.*

How's your joy? Does piety restrict your joy? Does guilt hinder your praise? As you ponder those questions, let me remind you of the verse upon which we have focused during the "Days" series, with which I conclude with this chapter.

So here's what I want you to do, God helping you: Take your everyday, ordinary life—your sleeping, eating, going-to-work, and walking-around life—and place it before God as an offering. Embracing what God does for you is the best thing you can do for him.

Romans 12:1

So far, we have explored how to offer our Sundays to Fridays to God.

- Sunday = Worship
- Monday = Work
- Tuesday = Small Groups
- Wednesday = Rest
- Thursday = Waiting
- Friday = Money

Today is Saturday. Saturday stands for a day (time) devoted to the celebration of joy. Honor God by pursuing joy in ways that bring Him glory. Emmet Fox wrote…

"True Christianity is an entirely positive influence. It comes into a man's life to enlarge and enrich it, to make it fuller and wider and better; never to restrict it. You cannot lose anything that is worth having through acquiring a knowledge of the Truth. Sacrifice there has to be, but it is only sacrifice of the things that one is much happier without—never of anything that is really worth having. Many people have the idea that getting a better knowledge of God will mean giving up things that they will regret losing. One girl said: 'I mean to take up religion later on when I am older, but I want to enjoy myself for a while first.' This, however, is to miss the whole point" (53).

God is not a killjoy!

Celebrate.

1. Him. (Reflect on His love and grace.)

2. Meaningful Times / Occasions / Events.

Then came the Festival of Dedication at Jerusalem. It was winter, and Jesus was in the temple courts walking in Solomon's Colonnade.
    John 10:22–23

We know the Feast of Dedication by its more well-known title, Hanukkah. Jesus celebrated Hanukkah. Likewise, He feasted at Passover.

3. Find joy in the "small things."

Play.

1. *Find* friends / *Be* a friend.

2. Play with your kids.

"If you've "slowed down" long enough to reach the end of this letter, let me encourage you to engage in a few more moments of rest before rushing off to your next responsibility. If you have young kids at home, why don't you consider sitting down with them and reading a story?" (Dobson 6)

Spread Joy.

Proverbs 15:30—*Light in a messenger's eyes brings joy to the heart, and good news gives health to the bones.*

1. Volunteer.

2. Coach.

3. Laugh.

4. Smile.

Receive God's Love.

Matthew 23:37—*Jerusalem, Jerusalem, you who kill the prophets and stone those sent to you, how often I have longed to gather your children together, as a hen gathers her chicks under her wings, and you were not willing.*

Jesus wept over Jerusalem before the religiously pious and explained to them that if only they would have opened their hearts to Him, He would have gathered them as a hen gathers her chicks under her wings. Imagine the joy of the chicks as they experience the warmth, love, and protection of their mother. You will be better able to celebrate, play, and spread joy when you accept the love of God. Yes, we are guilty; and yes, we have sinned; yet, even still, God loves us. He calls us into His wings.

As Oswald Chambers wrote, "We always know when Jesus is at work because He produces in the commonplace something that is inspiring" (Aug. 21).

As the Father has loved me, so have I loved you. Now remain in my love. If you keep my commands, you will remain in my love, just as I have kept my Father's commands and remain in his love. I have told you this so that my joy may be in you and that your joy may be complete.

John 15:9–11

PART IV

THE EXTRAORDINARY ALONG THE ORDINARY WAY

24

WHAT ABOUT GREAT?

Ordinary is enough. Ordinary is good. Ordinary will do. Yet sometimes your anthem does play; you achieve the 4.0; your effort gains the blue ribbon; and your professor scribes, "Great job!" on your exam. What then?

Well, just as it's okay to be good, greatness has its place. You and I will do well when we know how to handle the extraordinary, the great, the soaring heights. So then, how is it done?

When you experience and achieve the extraordinary, enjoy it. Allow warm tears to wet your face as the anthem plays. Hang the blue ribbon on your bedroom wall. Use the bonus to travel to that dot on the map you long to see. Skip. Laugh. Celebrate. Enjoy. Just don't rub it in.

When you win, soar, advance, achieve, recognize the victory as *extra*ordinary. That is to say, ordinary should remain good the next time you reach it. The undefeated champion team weeps in disappointment when they follow their perfect season with another winning season, except with a couple of entries in the *L* column. The husband complains that his wife's sex drive lessened even though the candles from two nights before still rest on the bedside stands. The boss accepts only the best even when the good consistently crosses his desk.

In his book *Springboard*, G. Richard Shell writes...

"Another force that can reduce Momentary Happiness is what psychologists call 'adaptation.' Something good happens—you get the new job or relationship you wanted—but then you rapidly adjust to your new circumstances, and these become the new baseline for judging how you feel. The glow of the new job or relationship fades, and you start to focus instead on the annoying way your boss talks or how your new romantic partner texts people while you are having dinner together" (42).

Such adaptation, when unchecked, leads the one experiencing happiness to lose interest in the now and exclusively focus on the "what if"—the ordinary and the excellent.

Another method to employ when the great occurs is the practice of intentional remembering. Enjoy the great while also remembering the joy of the good...

- The smile of your child as you handed her the soft-serve treat.
- The art of your son that he presented with pride where no lines are straight and you were forced to ask him to explain the masterpiece because you couldn't discern the image.
- The excitement of the completed task.
- The sunrise on the horizon.
- The moments of embracing your spouse's hand as you simply walked.
- The warmth of your cat on your lap.

See. Wasn't that a nice trip? Memory Lane leads to joy, especially when your fast track slows down.

Remember.

25

TOO NICE?

I enjoy sports. Not watching, particularly, unless my children are the athletes; but playing floats my boat. That said, I must confess that the best I achieved on the court of basketball (church league, at that) was "Most Improved Player." Need I explain? Think not.

At other athletic quests I achieved more success. Yet, still things didn't always go as planned. Several college friends and I gathered in the field for a game of flag football. I played a variety of positions, quarterback being the only one of which I know the name.

Due to my massive build—ok, that might be a slight exaggeration —as I ran down the field and collided with an opponent, he fell while I remained afoot. With the game continuing, I extended a hand. Sportsmanship? Yes. Good timing? Not according to my teammates. I was assured that I was "too nice" to play. Since then I have mustered up a game face and extended my hand somewhat less. In fact, some would tell you that my demeanor displays just a "bit" of competitiveness. Yet I continue to look for opportunities to congratulate or console the other team.

When you win, do you encourage the "loser"? When you achieve greatness, do you cheer for those who continue to do a good job?

The quaint phrases prove plentiful—"leave no one behind,"

"there's no 'I' in team,' "a chain is only as strong as the weakest link," and the like. Sap? Likely. Motivating? Hardly. Yet somewhere within those pithy sayings truth speaks.

By the way, coaches, don't bother with "Most Improved" ribbons. Ordinary is good. Calling attention to less-than, not so much.

26

THE DESCENT

I called half a phonebook. Only one jumped at the chance. I promise you'll catch the pun in just a few sentences. Faber and I drove to Temple—the town, not a place of worship, unless Thrill claims devout followers. We donned the far-too-tight blue suits, listened to the manhood-threatening news of how closely we would be attached to our respective traveling companions, and boarded the plane with no seats. At an altitude unknown to me, we advanced to the open door, looked down, and leapt.

Keep in mind that by the "looked down" part, we were committed. The aforementioned closely attached ones jumped with us hooked-on ones. I expected an unmistakable feeling of speedy descent. Rather, I felt more of a floating sensation. Falling at a rate of 120 mph, yet a false sense of remaining in one place. Thrilling! Awesome! Ordinary? No. But good.

Then he pulled the cord. Now the fact that we were falling was unmistakable. Minutes later, as my feet touched down, I realized that I was brought down to earth (pun intended again) from the exceptional experience.

Whether or not you have jumped out of a perfectly good plane, as the saying goes, you know descent. Flying lasts only so long. Has that cute habit of your wife's begun to annoy you? Does your husband's once so appealing outgoing personality begin to grate a bit now? Dust on the trophy? "Once-in-a-lifetime vacation" a distant memory, remembered now as you write VISA on the line just to the left of an extremely large number? Welcome to the descent. What now? Perhaps this formula will help.

Extraordinary – Extra = Ordinary

Notice the remainder. When extra is removed, ordinary remains. By this point in your reading, you see the value of the ordinary things of life. Solid ground after soaring high, recalling why the habit was cute, enjoying his enthusiasm, savoring the victories, and allowing souvenirs to tell the story of your extraordinary moments without robbing the ordinary of its goodness.

$E - E = O$

PART V

LESS THAN ORDINARY

27

MISSED CHANCES AND MEAN PEOPLE

United States Olympic marksman Matthew Emmons, certainly one of the top of his event, mastered control of his breathing, aimed, and pulled the trigger. Bull's-eye! Perfect shot. Gold medal!

He honed his craft with hour after hour of practice, outshot his fellow Americans and the marksmen of every other competing nation. He held the coveted prize—the gold. But did he?

Upon further review, the judges determined that Emmons' shot was flawless and perfectly hit the spot. One problem, however, it was the bull's-eye on the wrong target.

I'll call him Chris. Chris lived in my childhood neighborhood. Before that annoying fence was erected, I could run to his back door in one minute flat. (I actually never timed it.) He and I played on the same Little League team. When we weren't chewing our gloves and inspecting dandelions in right field, we took our times at bat.

Chris was up to bat with a perfect average—zero hits. Then the pitch raced toward the plate and by some act of God, his bat made contact—impressive contact. Base hit in the bag. With his fenceless run practice, he bolted to the base. You know what's coming, right? Maybe it was the act of God's archenemy. Chris ran to third base. Poor Chris.

Matthew Emmons is remembered more for his perfect miss. The other neighborhood boys and a few teammates taunted Chris relentlessly. The real tragedy is not the missed chances themselves. No, the real tragedy is what accompanies those missed chances—the mean people who rub it in.

Before you hit "send" on that email, know that I do not generalize here to the point of dividing our population into "good" and "bad," "nice" and "mean." I do, however, draw attention to the mean streak that raises its ugly head in each of us.

Think Lucy. I wonder if Charles Schultz ever drew good ol' Charlie decking that brat. Oh, wait a minute, I'm supposed to encourage turning the other cheek—aren't I?

People can simply be mean. I will now call names. *You* can be mean. (Hold off on that email one more time, please!) I write that accusation in reference to the meanness with which you treat *yourself.* The great Teacher summarized the whole of our purpose.

Jesus replied: "'Love the Lord your God with all your heart and with all your soul and with all your mind.' This is the first and greatest commandment. And the second is like it: 'Love your neighbor as yourself.'"

Matthew 22:37–39

Regarding the love that He urges us to direct outward, it is often in short supply. Here's why. It is extremely difficult to love those around you when you do such a poor job of loving self. We master selfishness and "me-firstness." Most of us (I'm married to the exception) like the biggest cookie.

We also enjoy the recognition that accompanies success. We know how to *like* ourselves. We, however, somewhere along the way forgot how we were encouraged to show ourselves grace, mercy, forgiveness —love. Jesus included that charge to self-focused love for good reason. We drain our supply of love for God and others when we fail to love self.

What hinders your love of self?

In the wise words of Bob Newhart, "Stop it!" In a comedy sketch, Newhart assumes the role of a professional counselor. A distraught women enters, seeking advice. She can't stop thinking about her fear of being buried alive. His professional advice? "Stop it!" Can it be that simple?

Note, please, I did not suggest that you "Stop it" on your own. Bootstraps often break when they are pulled. Take no shame in asking for help. The good God, an honest friend, a caring and skilled physician, a supportive faith community, and a motivating goal help the meanness lose its sting. The Beatles said it well; another Paul said it best...

And now these three remain: faith, hope and love.

But the greatest of these is love.

Love—far less than ordinary.

Love—find it, share it, keep it.

Love.

28

DIRTY DIAPERS AND DETERMINATION

Last century's comedian W. C. Fields declared that, "If at first you don't succeed, try, try again. Then quit" (phrases.org.uk). Fields modified the advice of Thomas H. Palmer in the latter's *Teacher's Manual*.

"'Tis a lesson you should heed,
try, try again. If at first you
don't succeed, try, try again."

Quitting has its place. One does well to quit smoking, lying, playing with knives, and attempting to spell *supercalifrag...* (Now how's that go?) It's also advisable to quit trying to live someone else's life. In most life arenas, however, heed Palmer rather than Fields.

When you come up short of good, don't give up. Persistence, as the saying goes, pays off, even when life stinks.

Just ask my oldest son. If you come to my house, I will show you the video. He points and pleads. His younger brother, just weeks old, rests comfortably on the floor and the camera rolls. With toddler determination, my son locks eyes with the camera operator (that would be my wife) and repeatedly declares, "Change! Change! Cha...cha... cha...change!" Caught up in footage-capturing, my wife misses the cue. So he persists, "Change! Cha...cha...change!"

Our youngest, still smiling, lay perfectly content in—well, let's say processed lunch. His brother knew that when life stinks, something can be done. Change.

Perhaps you are lying in processed lunch. Life's a mess and those around you know it. Hopefully, they cheer for a change, knowing that your life can be better. Thank God for those people in your life; and once you have, do your part. Don't give up!

Fresh starts—and clean bottoms, for that matter—have a way of making life more joyful. New beginnings grant us opportunities to live fully and to enjoy the sweet-smelling adventures that come our way.

Before you progress to the next chapter, pause for a few minutes and complete the following exercises.

Reflect on the current messes in your life and answer the question—

—What can I do to clean up this mess?

Reflect on the messes you survived and answer these questions—

—How did I experience positive change?

—What actions did I take?

—Who helped me change, cha…cha…change?

Now go thank them.

29

UNCOMMONLY GOOD

Why? W-H-Y. Those three letters combine to form one of the most difficult-to-answer questions expressed in the English language. And the meaning behind the word causes people of all tongues to press for an answer.

—Why didn't my marriage work?

—Why do I have cancer?

—Why the abuse?

—Why the pain?

—Why? Why? Why?

Whole books, libraries really, have been devoted to an attempt to provide substantive and meaningful answers. This is not one of those books. Every religion in existence constructs a theology in pursuit of the answer to such a difficult question, knowing the reason behind all that we experience.

God's plan? Karma? A foolishly lived past life? Dumb luck? You will hear as many answers, or at least attempts, equivalent to the number of those individuals you ask.

When seeking the ever-elusive solution to the riddle, we uncover the confusion between the words *ordinary* and *common*. Personal tragedy is common but not good. Suffering is common but not good.

Sin is common but not good. Those examples illustrate that *common* does not equal *ordinary*. Let us not confuse the terms.

Common, as I see it, refers to frequency; while *ordinary* refers to condition. Don't settle on common. Strive for ordinary. Excel at being good.

The late Dr. A. J. Conyers, a brilliant scholar, gifted professor, and man of deep faith, poured his heart into teaching. In many ways, he formed my process of thinking. He never attempted to indoctrinate but rather to educate—to open eager minds and challenge untested conclusions. On one occasion, as I absorbed his verbal tutelage, he expounded on the topic of sin.

He summarized theologies, philosophies, and conclusions reached by scholars and theologians—ancient and current—and then asked for our input. After much discussion, Dr. Conyers reduced the breadth of history and theology into one tangible conclusion. He offered the well-grounded thesis that sin is choosing the less-than-good. Simple? Yes. Profound? I certainly thought so. Over two decades later, that brief conclusion seasons my theology.

While I cannot answer the big "Why?" I can write with certainty that we inhabit a planet that is in short supply of good. Far too often we settle on the less-than-good. With heads held high, we can declare that we are less than ordinary when we fail for reasons out of our control.

Yet when we choose the less-than-good, we cheapen it. We too easily accept that things are not as they should be. Certainly they are not, but you and I can seek to improve those things around us so that they are ordinary. Uncommon. Ordinary. Good.

30

THE CUBE

Six sides, six colors, and hours of frustration. The time in which I even came close to mastering the Cube, surely created in the pit of hell, involved peeling and relocating colored squares. With a mixture of awe and jealousy, I would watch my cousin's best friend solve the Rubik's Cube with little effort and a wide grin. Eventually, my bitterness toward the boy wonder transformed into respect. He solved what, for me, was the unsolvable. He mastered the Cube.

Like the big "Why?" and the six-sided mind game, life often proves puzzling. Try and try as we may, questions and problems far outnumber answers and solutions. Yet, even still, like true Cubs fans, we cling to hope and trust that that "some day" will come. For Cubs fans, "some day" finally came in 2016.

Deep within our gut, that little voice, not to be confused with that Taco Supreme rumble, alerts us to the possibility of firm footing and priceless assurance. When the voice speaks, listen. Biblical scholars debate the meaning of Jesus' words about ears with the ability to hear (Mark 4:9). Whose fingers are in the hearing-impaired ears? God's or their own? I'll leave that question for you to ponder. Fingers, divine or human, aren't really the issue.

All of Scripture, especially the Gospels, cry out "Listen! This story's for you!" That little voice in your gut, your head, or the mouth of a good friend echoes the chorus, "Listen!" When you heed the advice, you will hear urgings to live well, let go of the thing that is robbing you of hope, surrender that vice which numbs you to real living, and "it's time for lunch." I hope that you also hear the words that Aibileen Clark, in that powerful film *The Help*, willed into her young listener…

"You is smart. You is kind. You is important."

Good.

PART VI

WORDS TO GUIDE

31

TOUCH AND TASTE—TWINS ON TANGIBILITY

Within my writing you will not find, unless you are already looking for loopholes, suggestions to pursue hedonism or approach life with a "to hell with it" attitude. You will, however, find encouragement to seek the tangible, to Touch and Taste.

Here the fun begins. Potential sits ready to pounce like a thought lingering on a tongue either not yet fully formed or temporarily blocked. Life awaits living.

Are you stuck? Does uncertainty restrain you like a chain three inches too short?

The day grows thin and the wind blows the trees as the animals rest and the humans wonder. Minds whirl as thoughts dance across the cerebral hemispheres. Left says, "Calculate." Right says, "Dream." They avoid true dispute yet reach no decision.

Here you must choose. Here in a mental limbo cage you determine whether staying will suffice or if you simply must progress.

I choose life. How about you? If you choose to join me in this pursuit, you will find two abilities, natural ones, quite helpful. I'll explain.

Mr. Nameless (his parents gave him one, but I forgot it long ago.) looked over my shoulder and concluded that the gift of drawing belonged to others. There in high school art class he suggested I lose the black chalk and pick up the tools for clay and plaster.

Through him I discovered that new mediums freed me to carve, form, and imagine without the struggle of every drawing looking like a cross between a bad attempt at cartoon and a style that in comparison made Picasso's pieces look like Realism. I quickly advanced from ashtrays for my non-smoking mom to thoughtful works inspired by my urge to create—short of museum-worthy perhaps, yet displayable. The difference? Touch.

Touch.

Look at that word again. In the second, and my favorite, telling of God's artful creative work, the writer informs us that "out of the dust of the ground God *formed* Adam." God got His hands dirty as He sculpted man. Surely, those who prefer a hands-on approach to forming images (no idols, please) inherited our Creator's preference. You hold in your hand (or peer at via your choice of screen) a book about getting your hands dirty. That said, hands tell part of the story.

The other part:

While teaching abroad I journeyed with newfound friends to The Giraffe Centre in Nairobi, Kenya. Eager as the youngest versions of humanity, I held the pellets of food ("one piece at a time, please") as an equally excited longest-of-necked creatures, with hilariously parted lips and far-reaching tongue, took the treat. That's when I noticed him. A boy of about thirteen, with a European accent of some sort, placed a similar pellet between his own front teeth and extended an invitation, one a giraffe eagerly accepted.

A gray and sloppy tongue captured the small bite from the teen's teeth. Having just experienced a far less intimate giraffe feeding, I knew that the boy felt the African slender giant's tongue in all its roughness. Ever been licked by a cat? You understand. I failed to consult a reference about the anatomical composition of the giraffe tongue. Nevertheless, even in all my biological ignorance, I surmise that the "bumpy parts" are the buds, the *taste* buds. The human tongue is covered with between two thousand and ten thousand buds.

Those tiny parts of the whole enable you to distinguish between sweet, salty, spicy, and bitter; they tell you when the milk out of your frig is too old and the bread stayed out too long. Perhaps you aced the Pepsi Challenge or won the Fire Ball War. Every time a slice of Moose's Tooth pizza meets my buds I am moved to a near divinely directed hallelujah. Thank you, my tiny friends.

While this book is about touch, it is also about taste. I well remember the vitally important times of decision-making. My fellow teens and I regularly addressed the all-important question, "Would you rather be blind or deaf?" As a stargazer and music devotee, I struggled to decide. While you ponder your answer to that query, I throw an added sense to the dilemma. Blind, deaf, or no more enjoyment of a slice at Moose's Tooth (you really need to try one!), Dr. Pepper, and chocolate chip cookies?

Taste.

Some would deem it an obsessive habit. As I have done for over a decade now, I record the title and author of each book I read; thus keeping a lengthy list of conquered texts. I read to enrich my trade, to investigate the opinions of others, and simply for literary pleasure. Through my reading, I commit to uncovering a plethora of skills such as gaining wisdom on leadership, engaging my imagination as the heroes outsmart the antagonists, and receiving advice on strengthening my interpersonal relationships.

I also discover the secret to making delicious waffles from scratch and the steps taken to create "Aunt Rena's Chocolate Cake" (best, by the way, served hot with a scoop of Blue Bell's Homemade Vanilla on the side; although a room-temperature piece for breakfast comes in for a close second).

Now it's your turn to engage your imagination. Consider, won't you, reading without leading, imagining yet never pursuing an adventure of your own, or learning to love yet remaining in your basement-based seclusion. Think of life filled with promising recipes that remain printed on the page and whose finished products never reach your mouth.

You do not need to imagine; do you? As you read these words, thoughts of missed adventures, unlived dreams, chances not taken, and what ifs cross your mind. Be careful. Do not ponder for such a length of time that memory leads to weighty regret and dampening second-guessing. Do, however, ask yourself why you left opportunities on the table and cakes in the book.

I believe, due to considerable reading, near-countless conversations, and personal experience, that permission rather than prevention survives into longevity. Tell me what I can do rather than suggest what to avoid, given the chance to influence me, especially in regard to teaching me how to live by faith.

Certainly "thou shalt nots" and hand slaps play an important role; but they, standing alone, fail to motivate. To illustrate my conviction, I invite you to join me for a journey on which we will explore an extensive selection of the words Jesus spoke to motivate His followers.

32

BELIEVE

Believe the good news!
Mark 1:15

The Son of God invited the people who listened to Him to believe. The Greek word there is *pisteno*. Using that word with intentionality, Jesus calls for more than mere intellectual consent. His words open a door to transformation, an active pursuit.

Your child believes in Santa (Warning: Spoiler Alert). I believe that the daytime sky is blue. The first belief is false; the second is true; neither is life altering. The good news, news that is true and clear, however, changes everything.

When writing to Jesus' followers in Rome, the apostle Paul explained the necessity of confession and belief. The intellect does not encapsulate the belief of which he wrote—"believe in your heart that God raised [Jesus] from the dead." The heart, in that sense, is the center of passion, the home of motivation. Touch and Taste starts with belief.

33

COME

Come follow me.
Mark 1:17

Here the Lord calls for a physical response to an intellectual and emotional commitment. The journey starts with a step. Step followed by step. Whether a pep rally cheer or war cry, motivational speech or ecclesiastical invitation, movement indicates response. Amens without actions merely tickle the ears. "I Do" promises without respect and love are as glasses more than half empty. Likewise statements of belief begin the journey of faith.

> *Then he said to them all: "If anyone would come after me, he must deny himself and take up his cross daily and follow me."*

Luke 9:23 1984 NIV

While the actions of self-denial are personalized, the theme ties all of them together—each person who chooses such actions discovers how God calls him/her to deny self and make personal sacrifices to do so. They, in the words of Paul...

...take [their] everyday, ordinary life—[their] sleeping, eating, going-to-work, and walking-around life—and place it before God as an offering.

Romans 12:1 MSG

Perhaps you count yourself among the number of people who would like to serve but either do not know where or do not feel equipped. If so, look for opportunities to discover ministries from the platform to the prayer closet in which to serve, to volunteer. Looking up the word *volunteer* in *Webster's*, you read the following definition...

"one who chooses freely to do something."

Digging further, you will discover that the word is derived from the Latin word *volēns*, a word that indicates willingness and wanting. The message? A volunteer willingly steps up and serves.

Three words of direction and three corresponding Scripture passages ready volunteers for your opportunities to serve.

1. *Find* your ministry.

There are different kinds of gifts, but the same Spirit distributes them. There are different kinds of service, but the same Lord. There are different kinds of working, but in all of them and in everyone it is the same God at work.

Now to each one the manifestation of the Spirit is given for the common good. 1 Corinthians 12:4–7

I remember the first time I read a label that surprised me. There was a reason; a word that I expected was replaced by another. Rather than the tag inside my newly purchased hat reading "one size fits *all*," the tag read "one size fits *most*." Whether for PC or legal reasons, the expected label was different. In regard to spiritual gifts, they are neither.

Neither fits *all* nor fits *most*. Before your conception, God knew how He would craft and gift you. At your second birth (Christians), the Spirit of God entered and came to dwell within you and brought a gift or gifts with Him. Those He gave to you. So your task is to find (discover) your gifts. How? Believe. Pray. Explore.

2. *Complete* your work.

Tell Archippus: "See to it that you complete the ministry you have received in the Lord."
    Colossians 4:17

Stick-to-itiveness. While you may not think it is a word, it is my understanding that it is now in the dictionary—and it does communicate. Once you engage in ministry, stick with it until God calls you to another opportunity.

Archippus is mentioned twice. Once here and once in Philemon. There the writer refers to him as "our fellow soldier." Apparently, Archippus took to heart the words of his church family in Colosse. We do well to follow in the fellow soldier's footsteps.

The more I hear it, the more I grow convinced that everyone's grandfather said, "Any job worth doing is worth doing well"—and for good reason—namely, it is true. Sloppy work and/or service holds no place in one's ministry of reaching and teaching. Complete your work and do it well.

3. *Keep* your head.

But you, keep your head in all situations, endure hardship, do the work of an evangelist, discharge all the duties of your ministry.

   2 Timothy 4:5

The Greek word for the phrase "keep your head" is *νήφω*. Translated literally, the verse reads, "abstain from wine in all situations." The Greeks used "abstain from wine" metaphorically in reference to moral behavior and sober thinking. Therefore, we conclude that here in the text, Paul instructs Timothy to commit to clear/level-headed thinking. In other words, don't...

- grumble
- fly off the handle

- lose sight of the goal (to minister)
- succumb to turfism
- give in to pride's temptation

According to the story, the Scotsman jumped into the Glasgow canal in order to rescue a bottle of Scotch that slipped out of his hand. He drowned. Commenting on the man's actions, columnist William Ward wrote:

"He gave his life for a bottle of Scotch!

What a person is willing to give his life for is an accurate reflection of his character, his values, and his self-respect.

What are you willing to give your life to? A noble cause? Your country? Your faith? Your family and friends? The safety of a baby or a small child? These are valid reasons for risking your life—for giving your life if necessary.

In reality, each of us gives his life for something—worthy or unworthy, eternal or transitory.

We are wise to commit our lives to a worthy ideal, a noble cause, or an everlasting investment.

Life is too important, too valuable, too precious to give it up in a frantic exchange for temporary satisfactions in the sea of selfishness—or for a bottle of Scotch in a Glasgow canal" (Ward 50).

Are you willing to deny self and practice sacrifice for something much more important than Scotch?

34

FOLLOW

Come follow me.
Mark 1:17

If the first step initiates the coming, a trail of steps indicates following. Here He calls for consistency. I leave it to other and wiser theologians to debate the accuracy of the views of Calvin and Arminius in regard to the perseverance of salvation. Meanwhile I, backed by personal experience and public observation, assert that a great number of "followers" camp out for excessively extensive stays in rest stops. I have pitched my own tent a time or two—or three, or four...

> *Then he said to them all: "If anyone would come after me, he must deny himself and take up his cross daily and follow me."*

Luke 9:23 1984 NIV

John Knox, a theologian of the last century, penned poignant words when he wrote that, "There are two ways to kill men: one is to rob them of life; the other is to rob life of its meaning" (Gilmour 170). Consider this question: "How will I follow Jesus this year?"

In order to keep the question always before you, I encourage you to keep it on your bathroom mirror, smart device, Google calendar, and anywhere else you will see it. Knowledge leads to implementation. Looking toward implementation, specifically to following Christ, we begin with knowledge.

How *do* I follow Jesus?

1. Recognize Him.

In the beginning was the Word, and the Word was with God, and the Word was God. He was with God in the beginning. Through him all things were made; without him nothing was made that has been made. In him was life, and that life was the light of all mankind. The light shines in the darkness, and the darkness has not overcome it.

There was a man sent from God whose name was John. He came as a witness to testify concerning that light, so that through him all might believe. He himself was not the light; he came only as a witness to the light.

The true light that gives light to everyone was coming into the world. He was in the world, and though the world was made through him, the world did not recognize him. He came to that which was his own, but his own did not receive him.

John 1:1–11

John introduces the gospel story with a sobering observation…

He came to that which was his own, but his own did not receive him.

Because Jesus resides in heaven at the right hand of the Father, you and I do not see Jesus in the flesh. Yet, we can still recognize Him. Through the presence of the Holy Spirit and the knowledge of the Holy Scriptures, we experience Jesus. He makes Himself known. I believe the words God spoke through Jeremiah to the Hebrew exiles remain just as true for you and me today.

For I know the plans I have for you," declares the Lord, "plans to prosper you and not to harm you, plans to give you hope and a future.

Jeremiah 29:11

While many believers take comfort in those words, as we should; unfortunately, the context of the message is often ignored. Notice that the knowledge of prosperous plans and hopeful futures belongs to God and Him alone—in verse eleven. That observation is crucial—for if only He knows and we know that He knows, yet we do not know, then we remain "in the dark"—so to speak. Something more is needed to be "in the know." Zoom out for a wider view.

"For I know the plans I have for you," declares the Lord, "plans to prosper you and not to harm you, plans to give you hope and a future. Then you will call on me and come and pray to me, and I will listen to you. You will seek me and find me when you seek me with all your heart. I will be found by you," declares the Lord, "and will bring you back from captivity. I will gather you from all the nations and places where I have banished you," declares the Lord, "and will bring you back to the place from which I carried you into exile."

Jeremiah 29:11–14

2. Discover where He is going.

Once you recognize Him, you know who to follow. From there, it is very helpful to know where you will be going. While many Bibles contain colorful maps near the back, Jesus did not draw them. The inspired word of God ends with the "Amen" of Revelation, chapter 22.

So, mapless, how do you proceed?

- Should you move?
- Which job should you pursue?
- Whom should you marry?

- Where does one find the answers to such questions?

In my former book, Theophilus, I wrote about all that Jesus began to do and to teach until the day he was taken up to heaven, after giving instructions through the Holy Spirit to the apostles he had chosen. After his suffering, he presented himself to them and gave many convincing proofs that he was alive. He appeared to them over a period of forty days and spoke about the kingdom of God. On one occasion, while he was eating with them, he gave them this command: "Do not leave Jerusalem, but wait for the gift my Father promised, which you have heard me speak about. For John baptized with water, but in a few days you will be baptized with the Holy Spirit."

Acts 1:1–5

Then the apostles returned to Jerusalem from the hill called the Mount of Olives, a Sabbath day's walk from the city. When they arrived, they went upstairs to the room where they were staying. Those present were Peter, John, James and Andrew; Philip and Thomas, Bartholomew and Matthew; James son of Alphaeus and Simon the Zealot, and Judas son of James. They all joined together constantly in prayer, along with the women and Mary the mother of Jesus, and with his brothers.

Acts 1:12–14

Wait. Pray.
3. Go with Him.

On September 23, 2013, militant suicide bombers entered All Saints Church in Peshawar, Pakistan. As a result, more than 80 people were killed and 150 wounded. When asked about his plans for post-trauma life, one survivor replied…

"What can we do now except...carry our own cross and follow Jesus?" ("All Saints" 3).

Rather than cursing God or calling upon the heavens for wrath to fall, our Christian brother in Peshawar pledged to continue to follow Him.

4. Keep going.

Endure, persevere, do not grow weary, continue, press on—why does the Bible contain those words in such abundance? Like any worthy endeavor, the most important pursuit, that of following Christ, proves difficult at times. Therefore, we need strength.

Paul understood this from firsthand experience. I find in his words, and I trust that you will, too, great encouragement and comfort as I keep going in my journey of following Christ. As you set out to deny self, take up your cross daily, and follow Jesus, keep Paul's words close to your heart and before your eyes.

I want to know Christ—yes, to know the power of his resurrection and participation in his sufferings, becoming like him in his death, and so, somehow, attaining to the resurrection from the dead.

Not that I have already obtained all this, or have already arrived at my goal, but I press on to take hold of that for which Christ Jesus took hold of me. Brothers and sisters, I do not consider myself yet to have taken hold of it. But one thing I do: Forgetting what is behind and straining toward what is ahead, I press on toward the goal to win the prize for which God has called me heavenward in Christ Jesus.

All of us, then, who are mature should take such a view of things. And if on some point you think differently, that too God will make clear to you. Only let us live up to what we have already attained.

Join together in following my example, brothers and sisters, and just as you have us as a model, keep your eyes on those who live as we do. For, as I have often told you before and now tell you again even with tears, many live as enemies of the cross of Christ. Their destiny is destruction, their god is their stomach, and their glory is in their shame. Their mind is set on earthly things. But our citizenship is in heaven. And we eagerly await a Savior from there, the Lord Jesus Christ, who, by the power that enables him to bring everything under his control, will transform our lowly bodies so that they will be like his glorious body.

Philippians 3:10–21

Therefore, my brothers and sisters, you whom I love and long for, my joy and crown, stand firm in the Lord in this way, dear friends!

I plead with Euodia and I plead with Syntyche to be of the same mind in the Lord. Yes, and I ask you, my true companion, help these women since they have contended at my side in the cause of the gospel, along with Clement and the rest of my co-workers, whose names are in the book of life.

Rejoice in the Lord always. I will say it again: Rejoice! Let your gentleness be evident to all. The Lord is near. Do not be anxious about anything, but in every situation, by prayer and petition, with thanksgiving, present your requests to God. And the peace of God, which transcends all understanding, will guard your hearts and your minds in Christ Jesus.

Finally, brothers and sisters, whatever is true, whatever is noble, whatever is right, whatever is pure, whatever is lovely, whatever is admirable—if anything is excellent or praiseworthy—think about such things. Whatever you have learned or received or heard from me, or seen in me—put it into practice. And the God of peace will be with you.

I rejoiced greatly in the Lord that at last you renewed your concern for me. Indeed, you were concerned, but you had no opportunity to show it. I am not saying this because I am in need, for I have learned to be content whatever the circumstances. I know what it is to be in need, and I know what it is to have plenty. I have learned the secret of being content in any and every situation, whether well fed or hungry, whether living in plenty or in want. I can do all this through him who gives me strength.

Philippians 4:1–13

35

DENY

If anyone would come after me, he must deny himself.
    Luke 9:23 (NIV 1984)

I met him in Kenya. He was a student in the Spiritual Formation collegiate class I taught. With his question, he, a Kenyan, caused me, an American, to pause. "In your country, what do people put first?" I had just explained my conviction that all people need to set their priorities. With chalk, in descending order, I wrote: *God, Spouse, Children, Church (Vocation).* In reply to his inquiry, I added a word at the top—above God, mind you. With white chalk on a green board, in bold letters I wrote, *SELF.*

The weight of the words found in Luke 9:23 proves no less heavy today than in any time in history since the Lord spoke them. The words are central to the understanding of what it means to be a Christ-follower, no matter the date on the calendar.

On January 26, 1943, my great-grandfather wrote a letter to his son, five months after my father was born. In part, he wrote...

"Men like you are not accidents and just don't happen—willy-nilly —; but are the results of an unchanging plan—of high purpose, of strong will, and willing self-denial and sacrifice."

Three generations removed, yet so emotionally and biologically connected, from that paternal letter, I read the words and think about how well they echo the call of Jesus. Strong will. Self-denial. Sacrifice. Homer (my great-grandfather) ran a general store and a postal service; yet in that seventy-plus-year-old letter, he crafted words fit for hermeneutics, alliteration and all. I could call them the Three Ss of living out Luke 9:23.

In order to make such a commitment to the Three Ss, you need to hear Jesus' words calling for such a thing. Thankfully, we find His words recorded in the holy Word of God.

Once when Jesus was praying in private and his disciples were with him, he asked them, "Who do the crowds say I am?"

They replied, "Some say John the Baptist; others say Elijah; and still others, that one of the prophets of long ago has come back to life."

"But what about you?" he asked. "Who do you say I am?"

Peter answered, "God's Messiah."

Jesus strictly warned them not to tell this to anyone. And he said, "The Son of Man must suffer many things and be rejected by the elders, the chief priests and the teachers of the law, and he must be killed and on the third day be raised to life."

Then he said to them all: "Whoever wants to be my disciple must deny themselves and take up their cross daily and follow me. For whoever wants to save their life will lose it, but whoever loses their life for me will save it. What good is it for someone to gain the whole world, and yet lose or forfeit their very self?

Luke 9:18–25

It is wise to intellectually grasp Jesus' call for sacrifice. Be assured, however, that intellectual grasping serves not as the ultimate goal. Rather, life application is the goal.

Verses 18–20 focus on Jesus' identity. The Lord draws His disciples in with a question. "Who do the crowds say that I am?" The crowds. Majority does not always equal accuracy. Who do the masses say I am? What is the common opinion of me? Once they provide a list of options, He (as His modus operandi) narrows the search. "But what about *you*? Who do *you* say I am?"

When we speak of Jesus as our personal Lord and Savior, we (rather than pronouncing selfish ownership) are testifying to our individual choice to follow Jesus. He never calls masses; He calls individuals within the masses. Like a child in the front row, Peter jumps at the chance to answer.

"The Christ of God."

Peter, a devotee of Judaism, grew in the knowledge that Jesus was the Messiah/Christ God promised to send. Upon hearing Peter's answer, which was correct, the Lord does a rather startling thing.

Jesus strictly warned them not to tell this to anyone. Verse 21

He strictly warned them not to tell anyone. Why? Shouldn't everyone hear that truth? Are we some secret club? Later, as exemplified in Matthew 28 and Acts 1, Jesus tells them to tell everyone. What gives?

Luke 9 is pre-crucifixion, pre-death on the cross. Professor S. M. Gilmour wrote…

"Jesus accepted Peter's confession but declined to have it made public until he had reinterpreted the popular messianic concept in terms of service, suffering, and sacrifice" (Gilmour 169).

Jesus calls for true, informed followers. He, in His grace, wants us to know what we are signing up for. No false salesmanship there! Professor John Knox wrote…

"So Jesus tells them not to use the words until after the redemptive event is complete and the church is fully in existence. Only those who have witnessed the suffering and resurrection of Jesus can be in position to know who he is and what he has done" (Knox 169).

There was, and there remains, grave misunderstanding as to the identity of Jesus. Teacher? Yes. Prophet? Yes. Kind healer? Yes. Oh, but so much more. The Messiah! The Christ! Yet, even still, not the one they expected.

And he said, "The Son of Man must suffer many things and be rejected by the elders, chief priests and teachers of the law, and he must be killed and on the third day be raised to life." Verse 22

"Rejected and despised, and *yet* the Messiah! Nay, rejected and despised, and *therefore* the Messiah!" (Knox 169) Once we know that Jesus was rejected and despised (as foretold in Isaiah 53), we receive more than a hint as to the demands on His followers.

Then he said to them all: "Whoever wants to be my disciple must deny themselves and take up their cross daily and follow me. For whoever wants to save their life will lose it, but whoever loses their life for me will save it. What good is it for someone to gain the whole world, and yet lose or forfeit their very self?

Why would we expect preferential treatment? Paul tells his readers the purpose of the Communion Meal. "For whenever you eat this bread and drink this cup, you proclaim the Lord's death until he comes." (1 Corinthians 11:26) The meal that we share reminds us that Jesus died. It reminds us of His sacrifice.

What will sacrifice look like for you? Dropping an unhealthy habit? Leaving a job that does not honor God? Living on less? Giving more…?

To follow Jesus, the would-be-follower needs to experience what I call a "Copernicus Turn." In the early 1500s, astronomer Nicolaus Copernicus formulated and expanded on heliocentric cosmology. That is to say, Copernicus identified the sun, rather than the earth, as the center of our galaxy. A "Copernicus Turn" is when one identifies *God* rather than *self* as the center of the world. As the opening line of Rick Warren's *The Purpose Driven Life* states, "It's not about you."

If at this time you need a "Copernicus Turn" or if you need to revisit your Turn (those two options should cover all of us), please notice the list of reading resources that will help you in your journey.

Readings from Scripture:

1. Abraham - Genesis 22; Hebrews 11:8–19
2. Esther - Book of Esther
3. Disciples - Luke 5:1–11, 27–32; Acts 2
4. Jesus -Philippians 2
5. Paul - Acts 9:1–31; 2 Corinthians 11:16–33; Philippians
6. Lydia - Acts 16:11–15

Books:

The Cost of Discipleship by Dietrich Bonhoeffer

Celebration of Discipline by Richard Foster

Simplicity by Richard Foster

Not a Fan by Kyle Idleman

Radical by David Platt

In His Steps by Charles Sheldon

The Purpose Driven Life by Rick Warren

In 1879 Russian novelist Leo Tolstoy sat down to write *A Confession*. In that work written during his mid-life, Tolstoy reflected on his journey away from religion, into hedonism, and finally into faith in Jesus Christ. He found faith by seeing it lived by those who denied self.

"…I began to draw near to the believers among the poor, simple, unlettered folk: pilgrims, monks, sectarians, and peasants. The faith of these common people was the same Christian faith as was professed by the pseudo-believers of our circle.

Among them, too, I found a great deal of superstition mixed with the Christian truths; but the difference was that the superstitions of the believers of our circle were quite unnecessary to them and were not in conformity with their lives, being merely a kind of epicurean diversion; but the superstitions of the believers among the labouring masses conformed so with their lives that it was impossible to imagine them to oneself without those superstitions, which were a necessary condition of their life.

The whole life of believers in our circle was a contradiction of their faith, but the whole life of the working-folk believers was a confirmation of the meaning of life which their faith gave them. And I began to look well into the life and faith of these people, and the more I considered it the more I became convinced that they have a real faith which is a necessity to them and alone gives their life a meaning and makes it possible for them to live.

In contrast with what I had seen in our circle—where life without faith is possible and where hardly one in a thousand acknowledges himself to be a believer—among them there is hardly one unbeliever in a thousand. In contrast with what I had seen in our circle, where the whole of life is passed in idleness, amusement, and dissatisfaction, I saw that the whole life of these people was passed in heavy labour, and that they were content with life.

In contradistinction to the way in which people of our circle oppose fate and complain of it on account of deprivations and sufferings, these people accepted illness and sorrow without any perplexity or opposition, and with a quiet and firm conviction that all is good.

And I learnt to love these people. The more I came to know their life, the life of those who are living and of others who are dead of whom I read and heard, the more I loved them and the easier it became for me to live. So I went on for about two years, and a change took place in me which had long been preparing and the promise of which had always been in me.

It came about that the life of our circle, the rich and learned, not merely became distasteful to me, but lost all meaning in my eyes. All our actions, discussions, science and art, presented itself to me in a new light. I understood that it is all merely self-indulgence, and that to find a meaning in it is impossible; while the life of the whole labouring people, the whole of mankind who produce life, appeared to me in its true significance. I understood that that is life itself, and that the meaning given to that life is true: and I accepted it" (Ch.10).

36

CONSIDER

Consider the ravens.
Luke 12:24

Consider how the wild flowers grow.
Luke 12:27

Perhaps I'll compose a word about "The Birds and The Bees" in another book. Here I focus on, consider really, birds and flowers. In comparison to F16s and Rose Bowl Parade floats, ravens and a field of wild flowers receive less "oohs" and "ahhs." Perhaps that's part of the point.

As I continue to argue for restoring the value of "good" and ordinary things of life, we can include ravens and lilies. How much time has passed since you last stopped to smell the roses? Lilies? Even dandelions? How long ago did you watch an eagle or raven soar?

I live in the beautiful state of Alaska. The forty-ninth state ranks among the highest in regard to racial diversity. Our state is home to over thirteen indigenous people groups. While each group holds unique and distinct customs and traditions, at least one tradition unites the various peoples—the tradition of respecting the role of the raven.

The native people choose to see beauty and magnificence in a bird many others simply ignore. While my view of the winged creature varies some from theirs, I greatly appreciate their example of seeing and placing importance on a creature for which our Creator provides. Consider that.

Consider, additionally, the wild flowers whose beauty tells a story of the sustaining God. A loving God. Over a dozen species of lilies exist, each with a simple beauty noticeable to any who pause to view them. From the Canada Lily to the Tiger Lily, the flowers show the creativity of the Crafter of all that exists.

One day as my wife and daughter met with a salesperson in the makeup department, my two sons and I attempted to kill time by riding escalators and perusing price tags. One such tag indicated that a shirt—nice shirt, mind you, with a different pattern inside the sleeve than the outside—could be ours for $248.

I noticed the tag first and asked my sons to submit their guesses. One guessed $50; the other said $75. When I revealed the true price, in surprised tone, my youngest son declared that that piece of cloth was priced higher than the amount we had spent a few hours earlier on my other son's brand new 22 caliber rifle—scope and ammunition included.

Expensive shirt! Someone, I assume, will buy that shirt. He will don an impressive amount of color, especially with rolled-up sleeves. Perhaps his shirt will even draw more attention than the one on his friend that cost $29.95.

Yet I tell you that not even Solomon in all his splendor was dressed like one of [the flowers of the field].

Matthew 6:29

Consider this. God loves you whether you spend $248 or $29.95

and the amount you spend does not determine His faithfulness to His promise to care for you.

If that is how God clothes the grass of the field, which is here today and tomorrow is thrown into the fire, will he not much more clothe you—you of little faith?

Matthew 6:30

37

LISTEN

Some pierce them. Some gauge them. Peter and Van Gogh cut one off; the latter his own. Jesus reattached one. Ears. On either side of my head, I bear one ear; that makes two, by my count. Below my nose and above my chin, I bear one mouth. It has been suggested that the usage of one's ears and mouth should correspond with the number of each, as in "You have two ears and one mouth; use them accordingly." That's advice worth heeding. We do well when we heed what we hear; however, since heeding requires hearing, heeding often remains undone since hearing is quite frequently neglected.

Pop Quiz! What did your spouse just say when asking you to pause from reading this book to listen? How, according to her own recounting for you, did her day at school go for your daughter? Or... How did God answer your plea? The caution to little ears to be careful about "what you hear" remains valid. So, too, does a caution to little (and bigger, likewise) ears to be careful to listen, period. Listen.

Her name means *star* and she became one. She was an orphan, yet she found a bright future. Beautiful in form and feature, she captured eyes, even the eyes of a king. Brilliant in strategy, she saved a vast number of people. May I present to you Esther, Queen Esther?

We find eight chapters of her story tucked in the Hebrew Scriptures between Nehemiah and Job. Twenty-four hundred years ago, the modern-day Iranian town of Shush was the Persian town of Susa.

In that day, King Ahasuerus (a.k.a. Xerxes) ruled the land as far east as India and as far west as North Africa. As the supreme monarch, one to whom all subjects bowed, he grew accustomed to unquestioned loyalty. Thus when Vashti, the queen, refused his drunken summons, his blood boiled. One hasty decision, one decree and one deposed queen later, self-inflicted loneliness shadowed Ahasuerus. Finding no pleasure in their king's daily frown, his attendants rose to the occasion.

Then the king's personal attendants proposed, "Let a search be made for beautiful young virgins for the king. Let the king appoint commissioners in every province of his realm to bring all these beautiful young women into the harem at the citadel of Susa. Let them be placed under the care of Hegai, the king's eunuch, who is in charge of the women; and let beauty treatments be given to them. Then let the young woman who pleases the king be queen instead of Vashti." This advice appealed to the king, and he followed it.

Esther 2:2–4

Whether by choice or parental demand, the number of young ladies in line for the throne grew and grew. Eventually, after six months of oil treatments and another six months of perfumes and cosmetics, Esther stepped into the king's chamber.

She was taken to King Xerxes in the royal residence in the tenth month, the month of Tebeth, in the seventh year of his reign.

Now the king was attracted to Esther more than to any of the other women, and she won his favor and approval more than any of the other virgins. So he set a royal crown on her head and made her queen instead of Vashti.

Esther 2:16–17

After any marriage, the bride and groom learn more about each other day by day. Most of the time, however, the basic background information about such things as birthplace, hobbies, friends and family heritage is shared much prior to the exchange of "I dos." Perhaps due to the fact that the king and queen skipped the dating and courting, one not so small detail about Esther remained undisclosed. Referring to her Hebrew roots, the biblical author wrote:

But Esther had kept secret her family background and nationality just as Mordecai had told her to do, for she continued to follow Mordecai's instructions as she had done when he was bringing her up.

Esther 2:20

While the marriage of a Persian king and a Jewish lady may have been unusual, it by no means was news of much significance—that is, until the arrival of Haman who we could fairly deem Haman the Boastful.

After these events, King Xerxes honored Haman son of Hammedatha, the Agagite, elevating him and giving him a seat of honor higher than that of all the other nobles. All the royal officials at the king's gate knelt down and paid honor to Haman, for the king had commanded this concerning him. But Mordecai would not kneel down or pay him honor.

Then the royal officials at the king's gate asked Mordecai, "Why do you disobey the king's command?" Day after day they spoke to him but he refused to comply. Therefore they told Haman about it to see whether Mordecai's behavior would be tolerated, for he had told them he was a Jew.

When Haman saw that Mordecai would not kneel down or pay him honor, he was enraged. Yet having learned who Mordecai's people were, he scorned the idea of killing only Mordecai. Instead

Haman looked for a way to destroy all Mordecai's people, the Jews, throughout the whole kingdom of Xerxes.

Esther 3:1–6

We learn early in her story that Esther, born Hadassah, grew up under the care of Mordecai, her uncle, following the death of both her mother and father. Fortunately for all the Jews of Persia, while Xerxes and Haman sat down to raise a toast to their plan to defend the dignity of the throne, Uncle Mordecai made plans of his own to protect his fellow Jews from said plan.

The only "hiccup" in Mordecai's plan was his inability to be granted access to the only one with the authority to stop the planned annihilation of his people; that one being the king. Mordecai did, however, have access to the queen.

When Mordecai learned of all that had been done, he tore his clothes, put on sackcloth and ashes, and went out into the city, wailing loudly and bitterly. But he went only as far as the king's gate, because no one clothed in sackcloth was allowed to enter it. In every province to which the edict and order of the king came, there was great mourning among the Jews, with fasting, weeping and wailing. Many lay in sackcloth and ashes.

When Esther's maids and eunuchs came and told her about Mordecai, she was in great distress. She sent clothes for him to put on instead of his sackcloth, but he would not accept them. Then Esther summoned Hathach, one of the king's eunuchs assigned to attend her, and ordered him to find out what was troubling Mordecai and why.

So Hathach went out to Mordecai in the open square of the city in front of the king's gate. Mordecai told him everything that had happened to him, including the exact amount of money Haman had promised to pay into the royal treasury for the destruction of the Jews. He also gave him a copy of the text of the edict for their annihilation, which had been published in Susa, to show to Esther and explain it to

her, and he told him to urge her to go into the king's presence to beg
for mercy and plead with him for her people.

Esther 4:1–8

The uncle, in other words, encouraged Esther to remember her roots and to speak up on their behalf—to give voice to those without one. In reply to her uncle's challenge, she reminds Mordecai that if she "speaks before being spoken to," she will certainly be put to death. Mordecai, not one to back down in such a desperate situation (if in any), retorts:

Do not think that because you are in the king's house you alone of all
the Jews will escape. For if you remain silent at this time, relief and
deliverance for the Jews will arise from another place, but you and
your father's family will perish. And who knows but that you have
come to royal position for such a time as this?

Esther 4:13–14

I am proud of Esther for speaking out on behalf of her people, but I am also proud of her for an action she took prior to speaking to the king. She deserves notice for her act of listening, especially since she didn't have to. Imagine her situation. Once an orphan; now a queen. Once a humble girl of no reputation; now a royal woman of world-renowned beauty. Helen of Troy has nothing on Esther of Susa. Esther now knew the "good life" with daily attendants; plenty, without want; and security. Certainly we would understand if Esther refused to listen to her uncle's pleas. Thankfully, however, her sense of "oughtness" trumped her natural urge for self-protection.

On the third day Esther put on her royal robes and stood in the inner
court of the palace, in front of the king's hall. The king was sitting on
his royal throne in the hall, facing the entrance. When he saw Queen
Esther standing in the court, he was pleased with her and held out to

her the gold scepter that was in his hand. So Esther approached and touched the tip of the scepter.

Then the king asked, "What is it, Queen Esther? What is your request? Even up to half the kingdom, it will be given you."

Esther 5:1–3

Then Queen Esther answered, "If I have found favor with you, O king, and if it pleases your majesty, grant me my life—this is my petition. And spare my people—this is my request. For I and my people have been sold for destruction and slaughter and annihilation. If we had merely been sold as male and female slaves, I would have kept quiet, because no such distress would justify disturbing the king."

King Xerxes asked Queen Esther, "Who is he? Where is the man who has dared to do such a thing?"

Esther said, "The adversary and enemy is this vile Haman."

Then Haman was terrified before the king and queen. The king got up in a rage, left his wine and went out into the palace garden. But Haman, realizing the king had already decided his fate, stayed behind to beg Queen Esther for his life.

Esther 7:3–7

Thanks to her willingness to listen and to act on what she heard, the Jews of Persia were spared the wrath of the petty and proud Haman. As you hear Esther's story, listen for your story. As to the life activity of listening, do you do well?

Each March thousands of Jews celebrate Purim. "Purim is often considered the most cheerful and colorful *of all* [emphasis mine] the Jewish holidays" ("Purim"). Purim celebrates the victory of the Hebrew people over their enemies who set out to fulfill Haman's wish to destroy them. Jews celebrate each year still—out of their thankfulness. Thanks to Esther.

God still uses men and women, orphans and those in power. He does this through them when they listen. God will use you when you practice the life activity of listening. Let us listen together.

On a day long ago, the Almighty Father spoke a word that remains true today:

This is my Son, whom I have chosen; listen to Him.

Are you listening?

38

BEHOLD

Behold, what manner of love the Father hath bestowed upon us, that
we should be called the sons of God...
1 John 3:1a (KJV)

Behold. I never use that word (except, that is, for when I just did while writing). Behold (Oops! I used it again.). Behold (once more, maybe) comes from the Old English *bihaldan*.

bi = thoroughly

haldan = to hold

Old or New, that "old" word communicates, powerfully so. In this world of Touch and Taste, the action of "bihaldaning" enriches life. When I thoroughly hold to something—I cling, I grasp, I claim. John invites his readers to cling, grasp, and claim the truth that the Father calls His followers children—sons and daughters. "See" works, but "Behold" seals the deal. Bihaldan that reality.

Jesus said, "Let the little children come to me, and do not hinder
them, for the kingdom of heaven belongs to such as these."

Matthew 19:14

Imagine the thoughts of the Lord Jesus. Confronting rebuking disciples so they will allow children access to Him, He opens His arms to the smallest human beings. What if He had more than newborns to teenagers in mind? Did He voice those words and think about how we, as adults, often act like children? By *children* there, I write not out of the sweeter side. Sara Groves voices words in her song, "When He Cries," to which every parent can relate.

"Looks like an angel when he's sleepin'
But he looks like Charles Bronson when he cries."

Behold, Jesus loves you when you sing in joy like an angel and He adores you even when your face displays your less-than-heavenly demeanor. He loves you with an everlasting love. Those who believe in, seek, and follow Him experience a reality like no other. The Christ explains why.

Being asked by the Pharisees when the kingdom of God would come, he answered them, "The kingdom of God is not coming in ways that can be observed, nor will they say, 'Look, here it is!' or 'There!' for behold, the kingdom of God is in the midst of you."

Luke 17:20–21 ESV

Touching and tasting connects one to God and His Kingdom, which is among us through His presence here now through the Power of His Spirit. That connection, fully embraced, leads one to...

39

REST

Come with me by yourselves to a quiet place and get some rest.
Mark 6:31b

Priority-setting and priority-living demand rest. One might assume that the disciplines (habits) of the Christian faith that require the most effort are those such as fasting, prayer, and service. I would argue, however, that the discipline for which we need much discipline is the habit of rest.

Sadly, the word *rest* brings to mind actions, or inactions perhaps, of slothfulness, lack of initiative, and the failure to achieve. Achievement and commitment to laboring for success claim a seat at the table of life; however, they also hog the chairs meant for spiritual reflection and rest.

Pop Quiz! Name the last time you did nothing *and* felt no shame for doing so?

We miss much when hustle dominates our days and weeks.

I wonder at what moment it started to tarnish. When did the gift of Sabbath lose its shine for the people of Israel? When they collected more than their share of manna? When they demanded a king so that they could fit into the model of kingdoms of the day? When did the exhausting labor like that of post-fruit-tasting Adam start to appeal to the people of God?

Perhaps we cannot pinpoint the origin of the souring of Sabbath, but we can calculate the damage. Ask the family practitioners prescribing medicines and life-habit changes. Survey your peers, asking questions about their level of dependence on caffeine. Check your blood pressure. We succeed at hurry and fail at rest. Eight hours a night equates to a fairy tale to most.

In 1939 the British government commissioned a poster designed to encourage her citizens to carry on with life as usual—calmly.

"Keep Calm and Carry On"

Over three thousand years prior, the spokesman for God descended the Mountain of God and presented two tablets (much heavier than the one in your lap) designed to encourage His people to carry on with life in a new way—restfully.

"Observe the Sabbath day by keeping it holy."

A quick look at the numbers of individuals taking sleeping pills, swallowing antacids, suffering from headaches, grinding teeth, and drinking enough caffeine to give an elephant the jitters—most people do not follow the advice of the poster or the command of the tablet very well or at all. In January of 2014, in the *Alaska Pulse*, I read a piece on finding calm. The article began…

"Your company's revenues are shrinking. Your kids need braces—and thousands of dollars for college just down the road. Your aging father has landed in the hospital again. And now that idiot driver on your left is swerving into your lane as he yaks on his cell phone. You might just snap.

Stress, when it's chronic or repeated, does more than unnerve us, it can make us physically sick. It dampens the immune system and dries out the digestive tract, setting the stage for disorders from irritable bowel syndrome to ulcerative colitis. It impairs memory and in extreme cases fuels anxiety. It can even gnaw away at the ends of chromosomes, accelerating cellular aging" (Singer 12).

In an edition of *TIME* magazine, I read an article on "finding peace in a stressed-out, digitally dependent culture." It reads…

"Researchers have found that multitasking leads to lower overall productivity. Students and workers who constantly and rapidly switch between tasks have less ability to filter out irrelevant information, and they make more mistakes. And many corporate workers today find it impossible to take breaks.

According to a recent survey, more than half of employed American adults check work messages on the weekends and 4 in 10 do so while on vacation. It's hard to unwind when your boss or employees know you're just a smartphone away" (Pickert 43).

Kate Pickert, reflecting on this plus the fact that "the average American teen sends and receives more than 3,000 text messages a month," concludes her piece with a personal reflection. She tells how she "started wearing a watch, which has cut in half the number of times a day" she looks at her iPhone and risks "getting sucked into checking email or the web."

And now, when she walks outside, she finds herself "smelling the air and listening to the soundtrack of the city." She adds, "The notes and rhythms were always there, of course. But these days they seem richer and more important" (Pickert 46).

While neither the *Pulse* or *TIME* article is based on Scripture, truth is truth no matter where we find it. And the truth is that God created us to rest in Him. After all, in the words of Jesus, *The Sabbath was made for man....*

The tablets of which I spoke earlier bore the Ten Commandments. As God presented them to Moses, He gave rationale for three of the commandments. The rationale He gave points forward for two and backward for the other.

Looking forward, God explains that those who refuse to make idols will experience the love of God *to a thousand generations.* Also looking forward, God addresses the value of honoring parents, explaining that doing so will lead to a life of longevity in the land. The unique thing about the rationale for the command to observe the Sabbath is its focus on history rather than any promise of future blessing. In other words...

The command to rest serves as a reminder.

Reminder of what? Reminder of two acts of God. To discover the first action taken by God, look with me to the first recording of the Commandments.

> *Remember the Sabbath day by keeping it holy. Six days you shall labor and do all your work, but the seventh day is a sabbath to the Lord your God. On it you shall not do any work, neither you, nor your son or daughter, nor your male or female servant, nor your animals, nor any foreigner residing in your towns. For in six days the Lord made the heavens and the earth, the sea, and all that is in them, but he rested on the seventh day. Therefore the Lord blessed the Sabbath day and made it holy.*

> *Exodus 20:8–11*

Reminder #1 = *God rested.*

The worn out and weak argument that "the devil never takes a day off so I don't either" voices arrogance and gives evidence that the one who speaks such foolishness is looking to imitate the wrong being. Would not the argument carry more weight that "God took a day off and, therefore, so do I"? You and your job/tasks are simply not so vital that they deserve your utter devotion. In the words of Alan Fadling, "Sabbath can be a weekly reminder that our work is not sovereign, but God is" (Feb. 21). Believe it or not, the world will continue to rotate on its axis whether you rest or not. Therefore, obey God. Therefore, rest.

Reminder #2 = *God rescued.*

> *Observe the Sabbath day by keeping it holy, as the Lord your God has commanded you. Six days you shall labor and do all your work, but*

*the seventh day is a sabbath to the Lord your God. On it you shall not
do any work, neither you, nor your son or daughter, nor your male or
female servant, nor your ox, your donkey or any of your animals, nor
any foreigner residing in your towns, so that your male and female
servants may rest, as you do. Remember that you were slaves in Egypt
and that the Lord your God brought you out of there with a mighty
hand and an outstretched arm. Therefore the Lord your God has
commanded you to observe the Sabbath day.*

Deuteronomy 5:12–15

God hardened Pharaoh's heart. God sent the plagues. God parted
the Sea. God sent the manna. In a word—God.

God softened your heart. God gave you your job. God answered
your prayer. God forgave your sin. In a word—God.

Sabbath reminds you that God does what you cannot do. God
rescues. Ken Garfield, over a decade ago, wrote…

"Faith is what allows people to emulate God and rest from their
works. 'Life is too demanding' for those of little faith, because the
inability to rest is the incapacity to let go of the illusion of control. The
constant need to work, shop, and meet demands can be a practical
denial that God is in control. Conversely, a spiritual discipline of
regular rest from the constant drive to check items off a to-do list can
be a powerful symbol of our trust in God's sufficiency" (qtd in "Where
We Stand" 42).

With the command, that is really an invitation, God ushers you and
me into a life of proper alignment. When we heed His command to rest
and likewise His call to "be still and know that [He is] God," we break
the chain of addiction to productivity.

Do you feel a sense of panic when you simply rest? Have you
bought into the lies that you are too important or that there is simply
too much to do to take a break? Take time to rest. Schedule rest.
Employers, give your employees time to rest. It is worth a mention that
the command to observe the Sabbath is a call to dependence, not to
legalism. Jesus healed on the Sabbath. Neither does the Sabbath
anymore have to be a certain day. Sabbath, understood through the

New Testament teachings, is a call to rest, not a set twenty-four hours on the calendar. However, too often followers of Christ turn those New Testament perspectives into license to skip a day of rest altogether.

The industrial and digital revolutions, while beneficial on many fronts, failed us. Progression and productivity replaced peaceful dependence. For far too many, the only time they will rest is when R.I.P. graces their tombstone.

40

ASK

*Ask and it will be given to you; seek and you will find; knock and the
door will be opened to you.*
Matthew 7:7

I carry a gun in my truck—a loaded gun. That fact may impress you or
worry you, but before you arrive at your conclusion, I must disclose
the type of the gun. In the words of Ralphie Parker, "a Red Ryder
carbine action two-hundred shot range model air rifle." Wide-eyed and
lisp-tongued, he voices his desire to all. Ralphie, the star of the
irreverent holiday classic *A Christmas Story*, sets his eyes, attention,
and dreams on obtaining a Red Ryder gun.

In a pivotal scene, Ralphie, at last in the lap of Santa after an
excruciatingly long wait, goes blank. Right in the lap of the jolly ole
elf, the boy's brain freezes and refuses to recall his desire for the air
rifle. As Santa, not so jolly this time, boots Ralphie down the slide, he
remembers his wish and promptly blurts out his request. Kris Kringle's
response? The same as Mrs. Parker's—"You'll shoot your eye out!"

Jesus loved story. The Master Teacher wove imagination and word
—well, masterfully! Recall the good Samaritan? Know the one about
the prodigal son? How about the nagging lady? There's a strange one.

In the story, Jesus depicts a judge as a thoughtless, godless curmudgeon who cares for no one, especially nagging widows.

Perhaps the well-worn phrase "persistence pays" comes from the rest of the story. The widow persists in nagging for justice. With no care to serve justice but rather to shut the mouth of the widow, the curmudgeon caves.

> ...yet because this widow keeps bothering me, I will see that she gets justice, so that she won't eventually come and attack me!

Luke 18:5

Jesus, as always, told that story for good reason—to teach a lesson, namely, a lesson on how to pray.

> And the Lord said, "Listen to what the unjust judge says. And will not God bring about justice for his chosen ones, who cry out to him day and night? Will he keep putting them off?"

Luke 18:6–7

Jesus contrasted a curmudgeon and the Creator. Unfortunately, however, many followers of Christ confuse contrasting with comparing. Do you find yourself asking God for your version of a Red Ryder all the while anticipating a boot down the slide or a refusal from a callous judge? Do you come to the lap of the Giver and struggle to articulate your request?

Others caution us to avoid praying selfishly and asking for requests that don't weigh enough on the "reason to bother heaven" scale. They have a point, perhaps a good one. However, we often ask too little. We might trust Jesus when He assures us that His Father will provide fish upon request rather than swapping it for a snake instead, but fear asking for the fish at all. The Good Father invites us to ask.

If you remain in me and my words remain in you, ask whatever you wish, and it will be done for you.

John 15:7

"God created the heavens and the earth"—sounds logical.

"The Lord parted the Red Sea"—makes sense.

"The walls of Jericho came tumblin' down"—no problem with that.

Even, "Jesus born of a virgin"—the Creator didn't need a man to pull that off.

Simply put, I find no difficulty in believing those truths of the Bible. Some truths, however, stretch my faith.

If you remain in me and my words remain in you, ask whatever you wish, and it will be done for you.

John 15:7

Time out! Here the stretching of my faith occurs. Parted seas, virgin birth—still no problem. "Ask whatever you wish, and it *will* be done"—Do you feel the stretching? I do. The Bible does not lie; Jesus tells the truth. Yet, when I read verse seven, I cry out echoing the words of the boy's father to Jesus, "I do believe; help me overcome my unbelief!" While this book is about God, not about me, I confess my stretching to you, trusting that you relate.

Without doubt I know the word "why" begins a large, if not the largest, number of heaven-directed questions. "Why God?" "Why God, did you...?" "Why God, did you not...?" With joy I declare that the God we worship fears not and angers not at questions of why. The Creator who formed you, giving you a mind and emotions, welcomes you to use them.

And so, today, we engage our stretched minds and emotions seeking to understand how verse seven proves true in a world so full of what appear to be unanswered prayers. Perhaps you squirm here fearing a lightning bolt or the like, or you are wondering if we have any right to question. If so, pursue an informed faith rather than settling for a pretense of faith filled with unasked questions.

A sound practice in studying Scripture is what is often called "testing Scripture with Scripture." Does verse seven stand alone or does it join a chorus of witnesses? Well, as we will see, verse seven is not forced to sing a solo. We hear companion words, also spoken by Jesus, just one chapter prior.

And I will do whatever you ask in my name, so that the Father may be glorified in the Son. You may ask me for anything in my name, and I will do it.

John 14: 13–14

Within the three verses upon which we focus we hear Jesus' clear teaching on how to access the promise of receiving when asking. Notice the following four phrases.

- "ask in my name"
- "If you remain in Me"
- "and my words remain in you"
- "to my Father's glory"

In My Name—

"Dr. Merrill Tenney reminds his readers that the phrase 'in my name,' was both a guarantee, like the endorsement on a check, and a limitation on the petition; for he would grant only such petitions as could be presented consistently with his character and purpose. In prayer we call on him to work out his purpose, not simply to gratify our whims" (Pg.146).

Your Father in heaven gives good gifts. His answer or "unanswer" may feel like stone or appear more like a snake than a fish. Keep looking; He will help you see more clearly.

Remain in Me—

Husbands and wives complete each other's sentences. One starts a thought; the other finishes. How? In an intimate relationship two become one. Sexually yes, but even more importantly, a mysterious knowing of each other's lives as, through honesty and vulnerability, husband and wife know, as we say, how the other's heart beats. Hear Jesus' heart.

Righteous Father, though the world does not know you, I know you, and they know that you have sent me. I have made you known to them, and will continue to make you known in order that the love you have for me may be in them and that I myself may be in them. John 17:25–26

"Prayer is a movement in a life relationship; it is communion before it is petition" (Blackwelder).

My Words Remain—

Do you want to know God's heart? Read His word and you will feel it beat. I find the words of wisdom from Frederick Buechner regarding the biblical story of Job quite helpful.

"Maybe the reason God doesn't explain to Job why terrible things happen is that he knows what Job needs isn't an explanation. Suppose that God did explain. Suppose that God were to say to Job that the reason the cattle were stolen, the crops ruined, and the children killed was thus and so, spelling everything out right down to and including the case of boils. Job would have his explanation. And then what?

Understanding in terms of the divine economy why his children had to die, Job would still have to face their empty chairs at breakfast every morning. Carrying in his pocket straight from the horse's mouth a complete theological justification of his boils, he would still have to scratch and burn. God doesn't reveal his grand design. He reveals himself. He doesn't show why things are as they are. He shows his face" (Buechner 55–57).

41

SEEK

Ask and it will be given to you; seek and you will find; knock and the
door will be opened to you.
Matthew 7:7

God does not hide. Why, then, do we seek? Our reasons for seeking vary with some motivations based on positive as well as negative attributes. We search because of our curiosity. We want to know. We search because we are restless. We seek because we know, just know, that we were made for something more.

We also seek if for no other reason than because we got lost. Or, if you prefer, "disoriented." The bride of fifteen years stares at the ceiling fan as she lies next to her sleeping husband. She wonders where the joy decided to hide and if it will return. The student with dreams of working for justice fails the bar examination and sees no brightness remaining in his future.

The teenager lands a role in her school's spring play, but not the lead role. The couple counts the days ("Just two months to go now.") until he retires, allowing them to catch up on lost time; what they don't know is that in three months, their physician will inform them that cancer is the cause of that pain in his abdomen.

Seek? Perhaps screaming is a more fitting option. If the songs of the Hebrew king serve as an indicator, ranting and worshiping sing a duet at times. (See Psalm 80.) Tevye the Dairyman found a way to seek with honesty. As he guided his limping horse, he spoke to his maker.

"Dear God.

Was that necessary?

Did you have to make him lame just before the Sabbath?

That wasn't nice.

It's enough you pick on me.

Bless me with five daughters, a life of poverty, that's all right.

But what have you got against my horse?

Really, sometimes I think,

when things are too quiet up there,

You say to Yourself,

'Let's see.'

'What kind of mischief can I play on my friend, Tevye?'"

(*www.script-o-rama.com* 03.08.16)

"Was that necessary?" While the act of seeking may not lead God to answer that question, it does indicate a positive step. Seekers don't seek with their eyes closed and backs to the One they pursue. Seeking indicates receptivity.

42

KNOCK

Ask and it will be given to you; seek and you will find; knock and the door will be opened to you. Matthew 7:7

    Knock, knock.
    Who's there?
    Lettuce.
    Lettuce who?…

Knock, knock.
    Who's there?
    Boo!
    Boo who?…

You know the rest.

As an anemic teller of jokes, "knock knock" ones rank near the top of my rather low-lying stack of jokes well executed. In a pinch, a "knock knock" pun goes a long way.

The use of knocking serves for more than gathering laughs.

Knocking can open doors. If, as purported, opportunity knocks but once; then most opportunities go unheard or unanswered. Therefore if you determine to *live a life worthy of the calling you have received* (Ephesians 4:1), you will knock on doors of opportunity rather than wait upon those singularly elusive knocks. Jesus commits to answering your knocking.

When I was younger (enough for the statute of limitations to have activated), I joined my neighborhood friends in the game known in Britain as "Knock, knock, Ginger." I grew up in Texas, so we knew not of that name; but play it nonetheless, we did. The rules? Very simple: Knock. Run! Repeat. Don't get caught! Do you find yourself playing "Knock, knock, Ginger" with God? You screwed your courage down tight and approached the door of the King of kings. He reaches for the knob and you run. The routine goes like this...

You: Knock, knock.

God: Who's there?

You: Mark

God: Be right there! (Notice the absence of "Mark who?")

You: (Silence. And not the stand-in-awe of His glory silence, mind you; but rather the "Never mind, I'll come back later" silence.)

We go to His door, ready to volunteer to "go anywhere You call" and then give way to second thoughts. We go to His door to confess our lack of faith, our sin, our pride, and then we run away in shame. We go to His door and...

I've never been to Turkey. I've hunted, stuffed, baked, fried, and eaten turkey; but I've never traveled to the nation tucked between the Black and the Mediterranean Seas. Were I to travel there, I would journey to the city of Denizli and find my way to the ruins of the ancient city of Laodicea where I would ask for a glass and the nearest tap. What is the temperature of their water? Lukewarm, perhaps.

Open a Bible and turn to the last book and go to the third chapter.

(Hint: It's the chapter that comes right before the book begins to sound really strange—*four living creatures had four wings and were covered with eyes*....(Don't ask me!) You will locate the story of a church in Laodicea. Here Jesus knocks.

> *Those whom I love I rebuke and discipline. So be earnest and repent. Here I am! I stand at the door and knock. If anyone hears my voice and opens the door, I will come in and eat with that person, and they with me.*

Revelation 3:19–20

Since Jesus knows that you and I tend to knock, run, repeat, He knocks and waits for our answer. You may have heard those words in messages about Jesus inviting people into salvation. Actually, that was not the original focus. He knocks, in those verses, on the doors of people who already follow Him. He knocks to get their attention so that they will open their doors to earnest repentance and commitment to continual obedience.

> *To the angel of the church in Laodicea write:*
> *These are the words of the Amen, the faithful and true witness, the ruler of God's creation. I know your deeds, that you are neither cold nor hot. I wish you were either one or the other! So, because you are lukewarm—neither hot nor cold—I am about to spit you out of my mouth.*

Revelation 3:14–16

When Jesus knocks, answer.

When you knock, wait; don't run.

If you're reading this in sub-zero Alaska, think about the comfort of a hot cup of cocoa.

If you're reading this in a desert of Arizona, think about the "ah!"

feeling of a glass of ice-cold water. Those taste much better than rusty-piped lukewarm tap water.

Knock. Wait! Enjoy. Repeat!

Listen for His knock. Answer! Enjoy. Repeat!

43

TAKE UP YOUR CROSS DAILY

Dwight L. Moody, the great evangelist, said…"Let God have your life; he can do more with it than you can."

Moody hit the mark with that first phrase—"Let God have your life." Clearly seen in Jesus' words is the call to surrender. However, you know how difficult that proves to be for each of us. Do you remember singing, "I Surrender *All*" on a Sunday only to surrender *some* on Monday?

Soaking in God's word, we will home in on each word of Jesus:

Take Up — Here we will focus on your *Willingness* to surrender.

Your — Here we will focus on *Personalizing* your surrender.

Cross — Here we will focus on *Identifying* your surrender.

Daily — Here we will focus on the *Frequency* of your surrender.

Before we dissect each part, let us approach God's five words as a whole. We do so best by observing the broader context of the five words, as told by Luke.

Peter answered, "God's Messiah." Jesus strictly warned them not to tell this to anyone. And he said, "The Son of Man must suffer many things and be rejected by the elders, chief priests and teachers of the

law, and he must be killed and on the third day be raised to life."
Then he said to them all: "Whoever wants to be my disciple, must
deny themselves and take up their cross daily and follow me. For
whoever wants to save their life will lose it, but whoever loses their
life for me will save it. What good is it for anyone to gain the whole
world, and yet lose or forfeit their very self? Whoever is ashamed of
me and my words, the Son of Man will be ashamed of them when he
comes in his glory and in the glory of the Father and of the holy
angels.

Luke 9:20–26

Luke tells us that the Lord's next words were *If anyone would come*
after me. Clear message? Translation—"I am going to suffer and die;
care to join me?" Reading the rest of the gospel story, we know that
while Peter's verbal answer was "Yes," his actual answer was "No." "I
don't know the man!"—Peter said in the courtyard as his Teacher
headed to His cross.

I invite you to keep "Take Up Your Cross Daily" in the forefront of
your mind. As you do, it will help you to understand what is *your*
cross. The words of a South African biblical scholar and a divinity
school professor will help you with your deciphering.

"The 'cross' is not the ordinary, human troubles and sorrows such
as disappointments, disease, death, poverty and the like, but the things
which have to be suffered, endured and lost in the service of Christ—
vituperation, persecution, self-sacrifice, suffering, even unto death, as a
result of true faith in and obedience to Him" (Geldenhuys 276).

"Taking up a cross for the disciple means the deliberate choice of
something that could be evaded, to take up a burden which we are
under no compulsion to take up, except the compulsion of God's love
in Christ. It means the choice of taking upon ourselves the burdens of
other lives, of putting ourselves without reservation at the service of
Christ in preparing a way for the kingdom of God, of putting ourselves
in the struggle against evil, whatever the cost" (Luccock 771).

With great ease, we can read such words as these and recognize their severity. The danger in our reading lies in their application. You, as well as I, hear stories of martyrs, saints, pastors in Iranian prisons, Chinese believers hiding in underground places of worship, "undercover" missionaries, and the like.

Their stories inspire and even impress us. The danger of this, however, is that their stories seem so foreign and out of reach; and, more often than not, we conclude, therefore, that that kind and/or level of denying self and taking-up-cross living is not for us.

How does a middle-class, employed, well-fed, non-threatened, free-to-worship believer take up her cross? How does a believer in a nation where Christianity, while at times laughed at, remains supported by law, deny himself? I believe that the apostle Paul answers those questions with exceptional clarity.

So here's what I want you to do, God helping you: Take your everyday, ordinary life—your sleeping, eating, going-to-work, and walking-around life—and place it before God as an offering. Embracing what God does for you is the best thing you can do for him. Don't become so well-adjusted to your culture that you fit into it without even thinking. Instead, fix your attention on God. You'll be changed from the inside out. Readily recognize what he wants from you, and quickly respond to it. Unlike the culture around you, always dragging you down to its level of immaturity, God brings the best out of you, develops well-formed maturity in you. Romans 12:1–2 MSG

The words of Paul here greatly enhance our ability to understand the five words of which I wrote—Take Up Your Cross Daily. Notice key components of living for God.

1. Take your everyday, ordinary life
2. Embracing what God does
3. Don't become so well-adjusted
4. Recognize what He wants
5. Quickly respond
6. God brings the best out of you

Figuratively speaking, everyone's cross takes a different shape. You may or may not know the shape of yours at this point in your journey. You do, however, know where to start—right here in Romans, chapter 12—with these six components of living for God!

44

TAKE UP

C. S. Lewis points to it when, in his Narnian tale, Lucy converses with Mr. Beaver. Responding to Lucy's question regarding Aslan, "Then he isn't safe?" Beaver replies...

"Safe? Don't you hear what Mrs. Beaver tells you? Who said anything about being safe? 'Course he isn't safe. But he's good. He's the king, I tell you."

George Bernard Shaw gives voice to it when, in his play *Saint Joan*, Joan of Arc converses with the Archbishop.

The Archbishop: Child: you are in love with religion.

Joan: Am I? I never thought of that. Is there any harm in it?

The Archbishop: There is no harm in it, my child. But there is danger.

***

With words such as "isn't safe" and "there is danger"—to what do the authors point and give voice? To the true nature of life for the follower of Christ. Reflecting on Luke 9:23, one commentator wrote...

"If we love God there is danger, the danger of a cross, the danger that life will be upset, that it will be loaded with the burdens of others, that it will be thrown into deadly combat with strong powers of evil" (Luccock 771).

In this chapter we concentrate on the two words—*Take Up*. Like Lucy and Joan, you have a choice to make. With the knowledge that "freedom from danger" and "promise of safety" are two phrases not found in any following-Jesus contract, will you yet still follow? Will you yet still take up your cross daily? The journey of following Christ begins with denying self and the denial of self is best exemplified through the action of taking up. Notice, too, won't you that...

The decision rests upon the follower.

One must be willing.

Jesus invites us to "volunteer to carry a cross" and "choose to endure for Christ's truth" (Buttrick 455). Listen to His invitation to His disciples and one of His followers' like-minded exhortations to later believers.

Blessed are the poor in spirit, for theirs is the kingdom of heaven.

Blessed are those who mourn, for they will be comforted.

Blessed are the meek, for they will inherit the earth.

Blessed are those who hunger and thirst for righteousness, for they will be filled.

Blessed are the merciful, for they will be shown mercy.

Blessed are the pure in heart, for they will see God.

Blessed are the peacemakers, for they will be called children of God.

Blessed are those who are persecuted because of righteousness, for theirs is the kingdom of heaven.

Blessed are you when people insult you, persecute you and falsely say all kinds of evil against you because of me. Rejoice and be glad, because great is your reward in heaven, for in the same way they persecuted the prophets who were before you.

You are the salt of the earth. But if the salt loses its saltiness, how can it be made salty again? It is no longer good for anything, except to be thrown out and trampled underfoot.

You are the light of the world. A town built on a hill cannot be hidden. Neither do people light a lamp and put it under a bowl. Instead they put it on its stand, and it gives light to everyone in the house. In the same way, let your light shine before others, that they may see your good deeds and glorify your Father in heaven.

Matthew 5:3–16

Who is going to harm you if you are eager to do good? But even if you should suffer for what is right, you are blessed. "Do not fear their threats; do not be frightened." But in your hearts revere Christ as Lord. Always be prepared to give an answer to everyone who asks you to give the reason for the hope that you have. But do this with gentleness and respect, keeping a clear conscience, so that those who speak maliciously against your good behavior in Christ may be ashamed of their slander. For it is better, if it is God's will, to suffer for doing good than for doing evil.

1 Peter 3:13–17

To all who read this today God gives an invitation to follow Him and live in devotion to Him, His will, and His ways. He invites. In the first century, Levi left a lucrative tax vocation, James and John left their father's fishing business, and Andrew abandoned his boat. In the twenty-first century, what are you willing to leave? In the words of Norval Geldenuys, are you...

"...willing to put [your] own interests and wishes into the background and...accept voluntarily and wholeheartedly (and not fatalistically) the sacrifice and suffering that will have to be endured in His service" (276).

The question raises eyebrows and perhaps even births butterflies in stomachs. What answer do you give? The verses known as the Beatitudes are relegated often to a category known as the "nice (or charming) words of Jesus." Let the rookie and the sourdough, however, hear the words again. Poor in spirit, Mourn[ers], Humble, Hungry, Thirsty, Meek, Mocked, Persecuted...

Perhaps humble and meek set well; for sure, the others hold no appeal. Why would *anyone*, even with the promise of blessing, pursue the others? Well, Jesus is not offering a menu; rather, He is stating the reality that when you follow Him, really follow Him, you will experience all these.

New Testament professor Darrell Bock provides helpful words for our current context. We do not feel the whip on our backs or receive prison time for preaching; yet we do know other kinds of suffering. Hear Bock...

"Discipleship means being a learner, a follower. It means that our attention is turned to how we can follow Jesus, not how we can make him follow us.

This means that we are seeking his kingdom, not our own. Materialism and the pursuit of power, independence, and security are probably the biggest obstacles to spiritual advancement. Everything in our culture from commercials to our education pushes us in the direction of advancing our [standard] of living for more comfort.

To pick up a cross means walking against the grain of cultural values, so that our own expectations and needs take a back seat to God's call. Some things we may have seen as ours by natural right may need to be renounced because they represent a subtle form of idolatry. The Spirit guides us into seeing things differently than we did before. Bearing a cross may mean leaving behind dreams created for us long ago by a citizenship we have now left behind.

So discipleship requires a renewal of the mind (Rom. 12:1–2) and a commitment of the heart to that renewal. It will mean intense involvement with God's Word and with other believers who are dedicated to growing in their faith. A disciple is never stagnant and never has the spiritual life in a mode where God cannot challenge him or her to a deeper walk. As Jesus has noted, it is an offering of the self in service to the Son of Man" (268–69).

Are you willing to walk against the grain and renounce some of your rights in order to follow? Are you willing? Will you *Take Up*? Peter, as we read, in a voice backed by experience, promises God's reward when you do. What reward?

Peter mentions...

1. a clear conscience Other voices in Scripture guarantee...
2. peace
3. assurance of strength Jesus assured the faithful...
4. comfort
5. satisfaction
6. the Kingdom of Heaven

Do those five (a partial list) sound appealing? Appealing enough to willingly take up your cross?

Lucy Pevensie chose to follow Aslan even with the knowledge that while good, he was not safe. Joan found courage, to love the religion—danger and all. To the Archbishop, she said...

Joan: There is always danger, except in heaven.

Oh, my lord, you have given me such strength, such courage.

How about you?

45

YOUR

Sixty-four years ago, Christ followers in Le Chambon, France, took up *their* cross. Following the fall of France to Nazi Germany, the people of Le Chambon resisted the foreign power—resisted, not with violence, but with faith. Author Malcolm Gladwell writes of their actions...

"On the Sunday after France fell to the Germans, [local pastor André] Trocmé preached a sermon in which he said that if the Germans made the townsfolk of Le Chambon do anything they considered contrary to the Gospel, the town wasn't going to go along.

So the schoolchildren of Le Chambon refused to give the fascist salute each morning, as the new government had decreed they must. The occupation rulers required teachers to sign an oath of loyalty to the state, but Trocmé ran the school in Le Chambon and instructed his staff not to do it.

Before long, Jewish refugees—on the run from the Nazis—heard of Le Chambon and began to show up looking for help. Trocmé and the townsfolk took them in, fed them, hid them and spirited them across borders—in open defiance of Nazi law. Once, when a high government official came to town, a group of students actually presented him with a letter that stated plainly and honestly the town's opposition to the anti-Jewish policies of the occupation.

Where did the people of Le Chambon find the strength to defy the Nazis?…They were armed with the weapons of the spirit…

…the strength granted to them by their faith in God gave them the power to stand up to the soldiers and guns and laws of the state."

What courage! What strength! What faith!

Yet, while moved by such faith, Gladwell offers a challenging question.

"But here is the puzzle: The Huguenots of Le Chambon were not the only committed Christians in France in 1941. There were millions of committed believers in France in those years. They believed in God just as the people of Le Chambon did.

So why did so few Christians follow the lead of the people in Le Chambon? The way that story is often told, the people of Le Chambon are made out to be heroic figures. But they were no more heroic than [others who acted in faith]. They were simply people whose experience had taught them where true power lies.

The other Christians of France were not so fortunate. They made the mistake that so many of us make. They estimated the dangers of action by looking on outward appearances—when they needed to look on the heart. If they had, how many other French Jews might have been saved from the Holocaust?"

While not looking for a cross to bear, when the occasion arose, the people of Le Chambon bore theirs—bore theirs faithfully. In the words of Bruce Metzger, "Only those who in faith accept the threat of destruction will find life" (NT15).

To borrow the words of Moses, *I set before you today life and prosperity, death and destruction.* That is the ultimate choice before you. Will you choose life? When we understand the scriptural truth that life is achieved through Jesus and acknowledge that Jesus' words in Luke 9:23 point the way, we grasp the fact that to choose life is to faithfully bear your cross. That begs the question, therefore—what is your cross? Jesus helps you pursue the answer.

Large crowds were traveling with Jesus, and turning to them he said: "If anyone comes to me and does not hate father and mother, wife and children, brothers and sisters—yes, even their own life—such a person cannot be my disciple. And whoever does not carry their cross and follow me cannot be my disciple.

"Suppose one of you wants to build a tower. Won't you first sit down and estimate the cost to see if you have enough money to complete it? For if you lay the foundation and are not able to finish it, everyone who sees it will ridicule you, saying, 'This person began to build and wasn't able to finish.'

"Or suppose a king is about to go to war against another king. Won't he first sit down and consider whether he is able with ten thousand men to oppose the one coming against him with twenty thousand? If he is not able, he will send a delegation while the other is still a long way off and will ask for terms of peace. In the same way, those of you who do not give up everything you have cannot be my disciples.

"Salt is good, but if it loses its saltiness, how can it be made salty again? It is fit neither for the soil nor for the manure pile; it is thrown out.

"Whoever has ears to hear, let them hear."

Luke 14:25–35

Considering the preceding ten and a half verses, Jesus' final sentence rings with clarity. Clearly, not all in Jesus' original audience, nor all reading this today, desire to hear such words of challenge. While not particularly germane to the story, the crowd count would be interesting to know. Notice the first two words of verse 25—"large crowds." I suspect that if Luke's source counted heads following Jesus' oration, the word "large" would have no longer applied. Eyes move side to side. Weight shifts from one foot to the other. Initial attraction turns to repulsion.

- Hate his family?!

- Hate his own life?!
- Carry his cross?!
- Give up everything?!
- Who does this guy think he is? I'm done with this!
- Martha, get in the car; we're leaving!

Speeches like this one filter the multitudes. Jesus never was one for hoodwinking. Perhaps He shot straight because He had a mere three years to complete His mission; or perhaps, and more likely, Jesus sought followers not fans. Disciples not do-gooders.

And whoever who does not carry their cross and follow me cannot be my disciple.

Luke 14:27

Perhaps the one who called for hand amputation and self-inflicted eye gouging throws you off course with the charge to hate. Eugene Peterson's phrasing of verse 26 pulls you back onto the road...

Anyone who comes to me but refuses to let go of father, mother, spouse, children, brothers, sisters—yes, even one's own self!—can't be my disciple. Anyone who won't shoulder his own cross and follow behind me can't be my disciple.

Luke 14:27 MSG

Refuses to let go. That phrasing aids our understanding of Jesus' word usage. Hate, in this sense, Darrell Bock explains...
"...carries a comparative force here. The idea is not that we should hate our family or lives, but that in comparison to Jesus, if we are forced to choose, the winner in that choice must be Jesus. He is to be loved more than anyone else" (401).

Bock is right on the mark. Do not allow his clarification, however, to cloud your mind, lest you miss the power of Jesus' charge. Jesus meant what He said. To illustrate the requirement to hate, rewind with me twenty-nine hundred years to the reign of Asa, king of Judah.

And Abijah rested with his ancestors and was buried in the City of David. Asa his son succeeded him as king, and in his days the country was at peace for ten years.

Asa did what was good and right in the eyes of the Lord his God. He removed the foreign altars and the high places, smashed the sacred stones and cut down the Asherah poles. He commanded Judah to seek the Lord, the God of their ancestors, and to obey his laws and commands. He removed the high places and incense altars in every town in Judah, and the kingdom was at peace under him. He built up the fortified cities of Judah, since the land was at peace. No one was at war with him during those years, for the Lord gave him rest.

2 Chronicles 14:1–6

During a time of rabid apostasy, Asa held his ground, trusting in God. He even held his ground within his own family.

King Asa also deposed his grandmother Maakah from her position as queen mother, because she had made a repulsive image for the worship of Asherah. Asa cut it down, broke it up and burned it in the Kidron Valley. 2 Chronicles 15:16

Centuries before the Romans instituted crucifixion, Asa bore his cross, even though it meant booting his grandma. The people of Le Chambon bore their cross of loving when required to hate. Asa bore his cross of integrity even as his own family rejected the Creator of heaven and earth.

What is your cross? I trust that you will recognize it when you see it. I know, also, that multiple crosses will arise in your life. Will you bear them? It may mean that you...

- Speak when it would be far easier and safer to remain silent
- Remain silent when you are tempted to speak

- Refuse to follow orders
- Submit to one who doesn't deserve such respect
- Defy long-standing family tradition
- Put yourself in danger
- Forgive the unforgiveable

46

CROSS

The year was 625 BC. The location was Jerusalem. The outlook was bleak. Into this scene a lone prophet declares the word of the Lord to an, at best, oblivious, at worst, hostile, gathering of lapsed followers of Yahweh. For his troubles, the Temple priest paid Jeremiah with a generous amount of lashes and put him in stocks. Faithful yet frustrated, Jeremiah levels with God. Give ear to the prophet's plea.

O Lord, you misled me, and I allowed myself to be misled.
You are stronger than I am, and you overpowered me.
Now I am mocked every day; everyone laughs at me.
When I speak, the words burst out.
"Violence and destruction!" I shout.
So these messages from the Lord have made me a household joke.
But if I say I'll never mention the Lord or speak in his name, his word burns in my heart like a fire.
It's like a fire in my bones!
I am worn out trying to hold it in!
I can't do it!
I have heard the many rumors about me.

They call me "The Man Who Lives in Terror."

They threaten, "If you say anything, we will report it."

Even my old friends are watching me, waiting for a fatal slip.

"He will trap himself," they say, "and then we will get our revenge on him."

Jeremiah 20:7–10 NLT

The year was 33 AD. The location was Jerusalem. The outlook was bleak. God's one and only Son declares the word of the Lord to an, at best, curious, at worst, mob-like, gathering of lapsed followers of Yahweh. The Romans, backed by the Hebrew religious council, nail Him to the cross. Faithful, yet broken, Jesus levels with His Father. Give ear to the Savior's cry.

"Eloi, Eloi, lema sabachthani?" which means "My God, my God, why have you abandoned me?"

Mark 15:34 NLT

The year is 202_. The location is where you live. The outlook is bleak. You follow Christ and speak His Name to an, at best, skeptical, at worst, mocking, co-worker refuses to listen and adds you to the "crazy" column. Faithful yet discouraged, you cry out to God. Your ears know what you say.

As we continue to parse this verse in order to comprehend Jesus' words, we focus in this chapter on the word *cross*. Take up your *cross*.

If you decide to take up anything, it is a good idea to first know what you intend to grab onto. Therefore, my aim is to help you in your quest to identify your cross. German pastor and theologian Dietrich Bonhoeffer wrote, "A king who dies on the Cross must be the king of a rather strange kingdom" (qtd in Treat). Adding to those words pastor Jeremy Treat writes, "A strange kingdom indeed. And the king who was glorified on the Cross advances his kingdom by calling his followers to take up their own crosses" (59).

Taking up crosses advances the kingdom—God's Kingdom. As those committed to advancing His Kingdom, believers submit to the Lordship of Jesus and, therefore, follow His lead in bearing crosses.

My old self has been crucified with Christ. It is no longer I who live, but Christ lives in me. So I live in this earthly body by trusting in the Son of God, who loved me and gave himself for me.

Galatians 2:20 NLT

We hear these words and understand them. But do we *comprehend* them? The difficulty so often is correctly identifying crosses.

Today, neither the Roman Empire nor their crosses exist. What crosses remain? The twentieth-century pastor Dr. Vance Havner answered in such a fashion...

"We are not bearing our crosses every time we have a headache; an aspirin tablet will take care of that. What is meant is the trouble we would not have if we were not Christians, the trouble we do have because of our identification with Jesus Christ in His death and Resurrection" (qtd in Hester 58).

"The trouble we would not have if we are not Christians"—that apt phrase alone thins the field. Too often, believers cry "persecution" fouls which, in reality, are more the bumps and bruises of life on earth for believers and non-believers alike. Regardless of one's faith-standing, people...

- Lose jobs to downsizing
- Lose loved ones to death
- Receive speeding tickets
- Dream nightmares
- Break their legs
- Raise defiant children
- Wed spouses who will choose unfaithfulness
- And so forth...

Do you remember Newton's law of physics—the whole action/reaction thing? His law applies to everyday bumps and bruises and it applies to taking up crosses. When you choose to take up your cross, you will elicit reaction.

Dan Fogelberg composed a song entitled "Along the Road." Take a look some of the lyrics.

"Joy at the start
Fear in the journey
Joy in the coming home
A part of the heart
Gets lost in the learning.
Somewhere along the road.

———————

Along the road
Your steps may tumble
Your thoughts may start to stray
But through it all a heart held humble
Levels and lights your way."

While I will not attempt to identify your cross for you, I will point you to the way to bear it. Look again to the final verse of "All The Road" that we read…

"Along the road
Your steps may tumble
Your thoughts may start to stray
But through it all a heart held humble
Levels and lights your way."

"A heart held humble levels and lights your way." Humble hearts recognize the wisdom of God's way and, therefore, do not attempt to avoid the cross that appears as he or she walks in it.

Will you take up your cross? I trust that the following words of Thomas Á. Kempis continue to motivate us to do so…

"…let us go forth together. Jesus will be with us; for Jesus we have taken this Cross, for Jesus let us persevere, and He who is our Guide and Leader will be our help. Lo, our King who fights for us will go before us. Let us follow Him boldly, let us fear no perils, but be ready to die for Him manfully in battle, so that we place no blot upon our glory, or diminish our reward by fleeing like cowards away from the Cross" (qtd in Miller 339).

47

DAILY

In *Your God Is Too Safe* Mark Buchanan writes,

"I did a funeral once for a lady who was a Christian, but few of her many children and grandchildren were. I thought I spoke the gospel clearly and boldly. Afterward, a woman came up to me. 'Thank you,' she said. 'That was so *nice* what you said. It was really *nice*. I'm religious, too. The family always ask me to pray for the weather when we go golfing.'

I reckon this: the idol of the nice god, the safe god, has done more damage to biblical faith—more damage to people coming to faith—than the caricature of the tyrant god ever did" (32).

"God isn't safe. God is a consuming fire. Though He cares about the sparrow, the embodiment of His care is rarely doting or pampering. God's main business is not ensuring that you and I get parking spaces close to the mall entrance or that the bed sheets in the color we want are—miracle!—on sale this week.

His main business is making you and me holy. And for those of us who love borderland more than holy ground, whose hearts are more slow than burning, that always requires both the kindness and the sternness of our God" (33).

Focusing particularly on the phrase "take up [your] cross daily," in this chapter we delve into the word "daily." Buchanan, backed by the words of Peter the apostle, is correct in saying that God's "main business is making you and me holy." Our pursuit of holiness is directly correlated to our willingness to take up our cross daily.

You may say, I'm not so sure about this holiness thing. Holiness sounds, well, you know, too holy. You may be in the habit, even if subconsciously, of reserving that word for God and/or things in and above the clouds. If so, embrace a more accurate and helpful understanding of holiness. To practice holiness is to commit to God, His will, and His ways.

God transforms you as you, in the words of Paul, *offer your bodies as living sacrifices*, which we accomplish by, to paraphrase Peterson, taking our *everyday, ordinary lives* and offering them to God. God accomplishes much through those who understand and, therefore, live the truth that true holiness is displayed when believers engage the world with God's love and justice. If I hear him correctly, Luke tells us that we must do that *daily*.

Why did Luke, unlike Matthew and Mark, include the word "daily"? John Knox explains.

"Luke adds the word daily. There is a sense in which this represents a "toning down,"…Mark undoubtedly means actual martyrdom. But in another sense the additional word adds to the rigor of the demand. Perhaps it is harder to "die daily" (1 Cor. 15:31) than simply to die.

Perhaps it is *continuing* self-denial which is so utterly impossible. Noble as is the martyr's heroic sacrifice in a great crisis, does it require as much of him as the necessity of steady and often lonely sacrifice of self over long years requires of another?" (170)

I've ridden a bull once. I've jumped out of a plane once. I've broken my wrist twice and both of my clavicals. I've had numerous stitches. With the exception of the jumping, I have no desire to repeat any of those events.

Compare two litanies of Paul.

Five times I received from the Jews the forty lashes minus one. Three times I was beaten with rods, once I was pelted with stones, three times I was shipwrecked, I spent a night and a day in the open sea, I have been constantly on the move. I have been in danger from rivers, in danger from bandits, in danger from my fellow Jews, in danger from Gentiles; in danger in the city, in danger in the country, in danger at sea; and in danger from false believers. I have labored and toiled and have often gone without sleep; I have known hunger and thirst and have often gone without food; I have been cold and naked. Besides everything else, I face daily the pressure of my concern for all the churches.

2 Corinthians 11:24–28

I do not understand what I do. For what I want to do I do not do, but what I hate I do. And if I do what I do not want to do, I agree that the law is good. As it is, it is no longer I myself who do it, but it is sin living in me. For I know that good itself does not dwell in me, that is, in my sinful nature. For I have the desire to do what is good, but I cannot carry it out. For I do not do the good I want to do, but the evil I do not want to do—this I keep on doing. Now if I do what I do not want to do, it is no longer I who do it, but it is sin living in me that does it.

So I find this law at work: Although I want to do good, evil is right there with me. For in my inner being I delight in God's law; but I see another law at work in me, waging war against the law of my mind and making me a prisoner of the law of sin at work within me. What a wretched man I am! Who will rescue me from this body that is subject to death?

Romans 7:15–24

To you, which account of struggles sounds more difficult to bear? Strangely, Paul rejoices, it seems, in the flogging and hunger yet grieves over his inner turmoil caused by personal struggle. Why?

Because while bruises fade and stomachs refill, daily struggles persist —daily!

In speaking the words *take up [your] cross daily*, Jesus presented a disturbing image. He, remember, had not yet hung on the cross. The disciples, the first hearers of His words, thought not of the Lord on the Roman tool of death; rather, they pictured thieves, murderers, and enemies of the state hanging naked and shamed. Imagine their shock.

Once the shock settles, another wave of heavy reality hits—Jesus speaks of a "Groundhog Day-esque" cycle of death. His words retain their truth today. You, if you choose to follow Christ, embrace a life of self-denial and cross-bearing, of accepting along with the blessings, also the consequences of existing as a child of God. Jesus and His followers told us that in advance.

If the world hates you, keep in mind that it hated me first. If you belonged to the world, it would love you as its own. As it is, you do not belong to the world, but I have chosen you out of the world. That is why the world hates you.

John 15:18–19

They will treat you this way because of my name, for they do not know the One who sent me.

John 15:21

Do not be surprised, my brothers and sisters, if the world hates you.

1 John 3:13

The begged question then is, "How do I suffer daily?" You alone can identify your cross; likewise you alone know how you suffer. We all, however, do share the responsibility to prepare ourselves for our daily opportunities to take up our crosses. In light of that necessity, I suggest some habits that will prepare your way and ready your response.

Daily Habits for Daily Cross Bearing

1. Pray before your feet meet the floor. (Psalm 119:147)
2. Say *your kingdom come your will be done.* (Matthew 6; Luke 11)
3. Prepare yourself to give an answer. (1 Peter 3:15)
4. Read the Bible. (2 Timothy 3:16–17; Acts 17:11; Psalm 119:9–16, 97–105)

Eugene Peterson writes…

"So how do we manage to live believingly and obediently in and under this revealed sovereignty in a world that is mostly either ignorant or defiant of it?

Worship shaped by an obedient reading of Scripture is basic. We submit to having our imaginations and behaviors conditioned by the reality of God rather than by what is handed out in school curricula and media reporting. In the course of this worshipful listening, the books of [the Bible] turn out to provide essential data on what we can expect as we live under God's sovereign rule" (422).

5. *Be self-controlled and alert.* (1 Peter 5:8–11)
6. Love others. (Matthew 22; 1 Corinthians 13; Romans 12:9–21)
7. *Rejoice in your sufferings.* (Romans 5)

As you wake from sleep tomorrow morning, you will enter into a journey of which you know little. You might have a great day and you might have a lousy day. You might feel like skipping or perhaps weeping. Whatever tomorrow holds in store for you, you can wake knowing how to prepare.

Therefore, since we are surrounded by such a great cloud of witnesses, let us throw off everything that hinders and the sin that so easily entangles. And let us run with perseverance the race marked out for us, fixing our eyes on Jesus, the pioneer and perfecter of faith. For the joy set before him he endured the cross, scorning its shame, and sat down at the right hand of the throne of God. Consider him who endured such opposition from sinners, so that you will not grow weary and lose heart.

Hebrews 12:1–3

48

SERVE

If you puff yourself up, you'll get the wind knocked out of you. But if you're content to simply be yourself, your life will count for plenty.
Matthew 23:12 MSG

Several years ago, during a rather difficult time in my life, I shared my thoughts and frustrations with a friend who cared to listen. I communicated to him my concern with the fact that others were attempting to make me fit into a mold for which my shape would not fit. Think square peg, round hole. Andy looked at me and said, "Mark, just be yourself." I'm sure my friend said more and that the other words were helpful; however, those brief four words set in motion my journey of self-discovery and healing.

A few days ago, as I read through Matthew 23, the memory of that conversation with Andy boarded my train of thoughts. I am thankful for those years' old words that remain accessible when their recall proves helpful. Do you relate?

A key part of Living the Ordinary is the courage to be yourself, to be content simply to be yourself. The translators of the NIV Bible phrase verse 12 as…"For those who exalt themselves will be humbled, and those who humble themselves will be exalted."

Do *humble themselves* and "simply be yourself" communicate the same message? It seems to me that they do. They do when the true meaning of humbling oneself wins out over the all-too-common misconception. For many, the act of humbling equates to groveling in a sheepish manner or a faked mental lessening of self—a pretending to be less.

Webster's does well in defining the word "humble"—"having or showing a consciousness of one's shortcomings."

(Go to gocomics.com/pickles and locate Brian Crane's 3/30/16 Pickles strip for a rather funny commentary on the "you can do anything" mantra.")

Ordinary people have shortcomings and recognize that due to some of them, achievement in all areas of life is an impossibility. At the same time, we recognize that achievement in many areas is not only possible but also worthy of pursuit. Humility allows for concentrated effort on achievable goals. Humility leaves the other goals to those fit to reach them and congratulates those who do.

Humble yourself and *your life will count for plenty.*

49

WELL DONE

I'm not writing about various ways to order your filet mignon. If I were, I would highly recommend requesting plenty of pink in the middle. But, as I said, no dinner suggestions today. *Well* and *done* are the first two words of the *man going on a long trip.* Jesus told the story.

Again, the Kingdom of Heaven can be illustrated by the story of a man going on a long trip. He called together his servants and entrusted his money to them while he was gone. He gave five bags of silver to one, two bags of silver to another, and one bag of silver to the last—dividing it in proportion to their abilities. He then left on his trip.

The servant who received the five bags of silver began to invest the money and earned five more. The servant with two bags of silver also went to work and earned two more. But the servant who received the one bag of silver dug a hole in the ground and hid the master's money.

After a long time their master returned from his trip and called them to give an account of how they had used his money.

Matthew 25:14–19 NLT

As Jesus continues the story, He tells of the accounting. In short, two pass; and one fails, miserably so. As I continue, and invite you to join me, on the journey of living the Ordinary Life, I keep this parable (often known as the parable of the talents) close at hand—or, better stated, hidden in my heart.

Why?

Here's why…

1. Jesus' story reminds me that He is generous.

Just as did the man to his servants, Jesus provides all that I need. No more and no less. I often pray the words of Agur.

> *O God, I beg two favors from you;*
> *let me have them before I die.*
> *First, help me never to tell a lie.*
> *Second, give me neither poverty nor riches!*
> *Give me just enough to satisfy my needs.*
> *For if I grow rich, I may deny you and say, "Who is the Lord?"*
> *And if I am too poor, I may steal and thus insult God's holy name.*

Proverbs 30:7–9 NLT

2. Jesus' story reminds me that He expects my best.

The master was full of praise. "Well done, my good and faithful servant. You have been faithful in handling this small amount, so now I will give you many more responsibilities. Let's celebrate together!"

Matthew 25:21 NLT

The master said, "Well done, my good and faithful servant. You have been faithful in handling this small amount, so now I will give you many more responsibilities. Let's celebrate together!"

Matthew 25:23 NLT

Why twice? Because the master said it twice. Check it out! He said the same thing (exactly the same thing) to two servants with different amounts. The "five bag" guy did not receive more praise; the "two bag" guy did not receive less praise.

I don't have to do *your* best. God expects *my* best. God is like a kindergarten teacher who loves teaching and the kids in class and expects each girl and boy to draw a picture of a house and smiles at each student's artistic ability with no concern for comparison.

3. Jesus' story reminds me that when I am "Five-Bags Guy" not to look poorly upon "Two-Bags" and to leave the accounting of "One-Bag" to the Giver of the bags. Remember—"Five-Bags" and "Two-Bags" both heard "Well done!"

4. Jesus' story reminds me when I am "Two-Bags" to be content— as in not jealous of "Five-Bags." Someone is always smarter, more beautiful, richer, more spiritually mature, a better pray-er, faster, more well-spoken, more popular, thinner, has a better six-pack, longer legs, fuller hair, knows more people, has read more books, builds better than you…you get the point. Yet, as long as I do my best, I hear the same "Well done!" The same holds true for you.

Live the Ordinary!

Let's celebrate together!

50

REMAIN

The Employee Tenure Summary from the U.S. Bureau of Labor Statistics reports that the median employee tenure for men is 4.7 years and 4.5 years for women. The US. Census Bureau reports that the median duration of residence in a home is 5.2 years. They state...

"The United States is often described as a geographically mobile nation in which 43 million, or 16.7 percent of the population, moves each year" (Hansen).

Obviously we, at large, are a transient people who find difficulty in staying still for even brief moments of time. Unfortunately, this obsession with rush bleeds into our relationship with God. Answers to prayers go unheard. Opportunities for impactful relationships get lost in traffic. Meaningful conversations stay unspoken. One author described the rushed reality in this way.

"Life is rushed and bustled, and in the jostle of competing interests always twitching at our sleeve and attracting our attention, spiritual things can easily get overlooked and lost. Seasons of devotion are shortened or crowded out" (Buttrick 717).

By the way, he wrote those words in 1952. Busyness, while a modern epidemic, is not a new kid on the block.

I am the true vine, and my Father is the gardener. He cuts off every branch in me that bears no fruit, while every branch that does bear fruit he prunes so that it will be even more fruitful. You are already clean because of the word I have spoken to you. Remain in me, as I also remain in you. No branch can bear fruit by itself; it must remain in the vine. Neither can you bear fruit unless you remain in me.

I am the vine; you are the branches. If you remain in me and I in you, you will bear much fruit; apart from me you can do nothing. If you do not remain in me, you are like a branch that is thrown away and withers; such branches are picked up, thrown into the fire and burned. If you remain in me and my words remain in you, ask whatever you wish, and it will be done for you. This is to my Father's glory, that you bear much fruit, showing yourselves to be my disciples.

As the Father has loved me, so have I loved you. Now remain in my love. If you keep my commands, you will remain in my love, just as I have kept my Father's commands and remain in his love. I have told you this so that my joy may be in you and that your joy may be complete. My command is this: Love each other as I have loved you. Greater love has no one than this: to lay down one's life for one's friends. You are my friends if you do what I command. I no longer call you servants, because a servant does not know his master's business. Instead, I have called you friends, for everything that I learned from my Father I have made known to you. You did not choose me, but I chose you and appointed you so that you might go and bear fruit—fruit that will last—and so that whatever you ask in my name the Father will give you. This is my command: Love each other.

John 15: 1–17

Within those seventeen verses, you heard a word eleven times. *Remain.* In the Greek language, the word is μένω (*men'-o*). John, the disciple and writer of Scripture, apparently loved the word. He wrote μένω and forms of it thirty-four times in his gospel and nineteen times in his letters.

You find it translated as *stay, dwell, live, abide, stand fast,* and *remain*. Certainly a word used over fifty times by one writer and several other times by others deserves our attention. In light of that assessment, I encourage you to commit a verse from John 15 to memory.

> *I am the vine; you are the branches. If you remain in me and I in you, you will bear much fruit; apart from me you can do nothing.*

John 15:5

Here Jesus articulates a beautiful "expression of the mystical union between Christ and the Christian" (Buttrick 717). He refers to Himself as the vine and believers as the branches. In order to understand the significance of those words let us look back on a chapter in John.

> *Don't you believe that I am in the Father, and that the Father is in me? The words I say to you I do not speak on my own authority. Rather, it is the Father, living in me, who is doing his work.*

John 14:10

The words translated *Father, living in me* in the Greek are πατήρ ἐν ἐμοὶμένων. Notice the final word—μένων. That is a form of the word translated *remain* in 15:5. From this language observation, we learn that the One who described our relationship with Him as one of vine and branches understood living as a branch as He remained connected to His Father.

Interestingly, indeed profoundly, in the ancient text of the prophet Isaiah we discover a prophetic word foretelling the arrival of Jesus.

> *A shoot will come up from the stump of Jesse;*
>   *from his roots a Branch will bear fruit.*
>   *The Spirit of the Lord will rest on him—*
>   *the Spirit of wisdom and of understanding,*

the Spirit of counsel and of might,
the Spirit of the knowledge and fear of the Lord—
and he will delight in the fear of the Lord.
He will not judge by what he sees with his eyes,
or decide by what he hears with his ears.

Isaiah 11:1–3

Jesus, the Branch, came to this world in love and, as He confessed in John 14, drew sustenance and strength from God the Father. Therefore, as Jesus calls His followers to live as branches, He does so out of a voice of experience. He daily spent time with His Father and because of that intimate connection, was able to reveal Him perfectly and serve Him completely.

As you travel this journey with Christ, I encourage you to focus more on *Be* rather than *Do.* What does that mean? It means that I urge you to focus on who you are in Christ before you concentrate on what you do for Christ. Identity before productivity. Consider what Leon Morris writes about this...

"The roles of Christ and of his followers are not to be confused. But there is a mutual indwelling, and this is the condition of fruitfulness. Those who so abide in Christ and have Christ abiding in them keep on bearing fruit in quantity. The verse concludes with an emphatic declaration of human helplessness apart from Christ. In isolation from him no spiritual achievement is possible. For the complementary truth compare 'I can do everything through him who gives me strength' (Phil. 4:13)" (595–596).

I believe that far too many Christ-followers wear themselves out in pursuing a good thing at the expense of the best thing. They try exceedingly hard to do great things for God—pray sincerely, read the Bible regularly, volunteer without fail—yet wear themselves out because they are doing so fueled by their own source of energy rather than the Spirit of Christ's divine power.

The longtime pastor and former Chaplain of the United States Senate, Lloyd Ogilvie, reflected on the apostle Peter's struggle with such tiresome religious effort. In his book *Ask Him Anything* Ogilvie writes...

"A few weeks ago I was talking to a friend of mine about his experience as a High School football coach. He told me that one of the most difficult skills to teach his defensive players is to be patient in engaging the offensive player. If, as I understand it a defensive player engages the ball carrier, for example, by charging too quickly the runner will more easily avoid the tackle" (226).

Football fan or not, you see the parallel with the Christian life. So often we commit to tackling a project or endeavor so quickly that we get burned, or at least burned out.

In our busyness, especially our religious busyness, we need to slow the pace and *Be*. The *doing* will come; first embrace the *being*.

I am the vine; you are the branches. If you remain in me and I in you, you will bear much fruit; apart from me you can do nothing.

John 15:5

51

WHAT IS THAT TO YOU?

Jesus spoke to Peter.

'Very truly I tell you, when you were younger you dressed yourself and wen where you wanted; but when you are old you will stretch out your hands, and someone else will dress you and lead you where you do not want to go." Jesus said this to indicate the kind of death by which Peter would glorify God. Then he said to him 'Follow me!' Peter turned and saw that the disciple whom Jesus loved was following them. (This was the one who leaned back against Jesus at the supper and had said, 'Lord, who is going to betray you?'). When Peter saw him, he asked, 'Lord, what about him?'

John 21:18-21

John McKinnon writes…

"The final task of human and Christian maturity is to arrive at a place of interior serenity—to find release from the restless desires learnt from others, which give rise, in their turn, to constant and instinctive comparison, envy, competitiveness, rivalry, struggle and even veiled or overt violence.

Peter's question: 'What about him?' seems to have been an instance of that human tendency to comparison and rivalry. Jesus' response to Peter was an invitation (and an empowerment?) to move beyond 'looking over the shoulder' at the other, and to keep focused simply on following Jesus: 'Follow me'.

In fact, the faithful following of Jesus leads to the release of the true self, the self created in the image of God and christened at baptism. The deep human desires of the true self are the desires, too, of Jesus. As disciples draw ever closer to Jesus in love, they come to acquire his vision and desires. Life becomes no longer a constant competition with others but a serenely powerful commitment to love, justice, compassion and forgiveness" (johnmckinnon.org).

Reinstated Peter felt the pull of comparison. Did he dislike John for his more faithful behavior? Perhaps envy rather than dislike; yet, even still, more like dislike for himself than anything to do with John. If, rather than John, Andrew caught Peter's eye, he still would have asked the same question of Jesus, "Lord, what about him?" Responding to the question with his own question, Jesus asked,

If I want him to remain alive until I return, what is that to you? You must follow me.

John 21:22

Excepting the apostle's closing thoughts, the twenty-first chapter and, therefore, the book of John concludes with Jesus' question yet unanswered. How fitting! John, in his gospel and letters, articulates his reasons for writing.

For example:

But these are written that you may believe that Jesus is the Messiah, the Son of God, and that by believing you may have life in his name.

John 20:31

And:

We proclaim to you what we have seen and heard, so that you also may have fellowship with us. And our fellowship is with the Father and with his Son, Jesus Christ.

1 John 1:3

And:

I write these things to you who believe in the name of the Son of God so that you may know that you have eternal life.

1 John 5:13

Jesus' question to Peter echoes in our ears. His question is to each individual who will listen. Jesus died for the world and the world is composed of individuals—individuals faced with the question of "What will *I* do?"

When Jesus asked, did Peter's mind return to that day on the sea, to the tossing waves, to his Lord ignoring gravity, to his own gravity-defying walk—to his sinking? There on Sea of Galilee he sank because he took his eyes off of Jesus. He could not afford to do that again by placing his eyes on John.

First grade teachers and "corralers" of Tigers, Bobcats, Bears, and Wolves (of the Cub Scout variety) understand crowd control. The veterans of classroom and den meeting environments voice a very simple phrase…"Eyes on me!"

They know the value of undivided attention.

So did Jesus.

"What is that to you?"

PART VII

SPEAK UP

52

SEALING THE DEAL

Insurance salespeople remind us of the unavoidable nature of death. Social media addicts eagerly share the latest world event, new discovery, and videos of cute children doing silly things. Prophets, true and false, speak of impending doom. Evangelicals passionately tell the story of a loving God and His good gift of salvation. Convinced people speak up. I have accomplished my goal if you, still reading after fifty-one chapters, are convinced of the significance of the ordinary things of life.

I now invite you to spread the word. Tell the story. Tell *your* story. Those of us categorized somewhere among the "normal" people can tell of the ordinary, extraordinary, and less-than-ordinary events of our lives. I am convinced, taught by experience, that mere ordinary stories deserve telling. You motivate those who think that because their lives do not capture headlines or don't attract a near-endless number of social media followers that they matter, that their everyday, ordinary lives have significance.

I hold in my hand a Bic Pro Plus (Yes, I originally wrote this with a pencil.) and form sentences from words. I write these sentences on a legal pad—yellow, if you're curious—which rests on top of a table as fluorescent bulbs team with sunlight illuminate my task.

While I know who created the sun, I possess no knowledge of the person behind the idea for Bic, legal pads, or bulbs. (That last one might be Thomas Edison; yet I think others of his same generation deserve their own share of the credit.) Nevertheless, to return to my point, most of the amenities and tools of my life, trade, and hobbies exist because of some long-forgotten or never-known ordinary person. Here I lift up a written cheer to those women and men. To those long-forgotten and never-known, I say "Thank you!" For that matter, to you who read this book, "Thank you!" for the ordinary and good things that I will never know you do.

53

A WORD TO PARENTS

My wife and I are raising our daughter and two sons. At the time of this writing, they are eighteen, sixteen, and fourteen. Next to my Lord and my wife, our three children are the true loves of my life. Not long ago, I composed "A Poem For My Wife." The third stanza reads as such:

"She guides her children with love.

Seeking to see them succeed.

In life; yes, but above

All else in the real need—

The path He chose for them to lead."

I join her in that pursuit. We encourage our children to achieve much, to achieve good. In the words of Max Lucado "It is not enough…to do well. [We] want to do good" (4).

She and I are aided in our parental quest by our experiences as children. I will tell you part of my story. In the room of each of my sons, a frame horizontally presents the likenesses of six generations of Goodman men—Thomas Kelly, Homer Hanniman Helmuth, Thomas Kime, John Thomas, Mark Thomas, and my sons. The photos remind me of a legacy, one I pledge to continue.

My father, John, and mother, Lynn, raised my two sisters and me in a home of love and encouragement in a home where achievement was celebrated and not only when those accomplishments were extraordinary. Ordinary was praised rather than cheapened by comparison to great and beyond.

My sisters and I achieved some great things—high GPAs, athletic victories, thespian awards, Eagle Scout, and the like (not much success in music, however—no good genes there). We also lost games, "bombed" some tests, tested our parents' patience, quit when we should have persisted—and, through it all, we were loved. I heard in their words of support, encouragement similar to that of which I wrote earlier…"You is good. You is kind. You is important"—although my mother would never allow the faulty grammar. Thank you for that, Mom—seriously.

54

A WORD TO TEACHERS

Stop reading for a few moments after you finish this next sentence. Reflect on the teachers who most impacted your life in school, church, art pursuits, and recall why.

No, seriously, stop reading.

Here you are reflecting...

What did you discover? Who came to mind? Most likely, as I am doing as I write, you thought of the teachers who you respected most as well as those you liked least. The teachers, instructors, pastors, coaches that earn our respect poured their lives into us; and while motivating us to attempt *great* things, continued to encourage us when we achieved *good* things. The least-liked either expected too much or simply didn't care one way or another.

If you teach, instruct, coach, counsel, inspire, train, or have influence in anyone's life, do so with an appreciation for the good and a respect for the ordinary. When you preach, urge rather than angrily rebuke. When you instruct, demonstrate rather than demand. When you coach, motivate rather than humiliate. When you teach, educate rather than test. When you counsel, pursue healing rather pushing for answers.

Whenever you hold influence, treat those whom you affect as ordinary people capable of extraordinary things and as extraordinary people doing ordinary things. Ordinarily praise ordinary.

55

MORE TOES

Toes. Remember the pinky toe collision? Perhaps rather than the result of a nighttime collision, your toes hurt because I stepped on them. Hopefully, however, in such stomping, I have softened some hearts and rewritten some life-achievement charts.

Far too many men and women, boys and girls, are stuck—stuck in the muck of self-doubt and personalized discouragement. Enough is enough! I devoted time to the writing of this book to reframe the picture of expectation. I have no desire to lower expectations or discourage extraordinary accomplishments.

I do, however, urge you to consider the damage done to others and yourself when we highlight the great and forget the good, when we praise the extraordinary and ignore the ordinary.

On the next pages you will find four exercises that will help you to undo some of the damage. Devote some time to completing them.

EXERCISE 1

Exercise #1

Review a timespan of your choice (week, month, year, etc.) and record *your* accomplishments of which you are most proud.

Exercise #2

Review a timespan of your choice (week, month, year, etc.) and record the accomplishments *of others* (family, children, students, etc.) that you consider worthy of note.

Exercise #3

Review a timespan of your choice (week, month, year, etc.) and record *your* accomplishments of which you are *least* proud or the failures that you *most regret*.

Exercise #4—Part One

Enjoy time celebrating the ordinary and extraordinary you recorded in Exercise #1.

Exercise #4—Part Two

Tell some (or all) of those whose accomplishments you recorded in Exercise #2 how/why you think their accomplishments are significant.

Exercise #4—Part Three

Celebrate the less-than-ordinary achievements you recorded in Exercise #3 and forgive yourself for the most-regretted failures you recorded in the same exercise.

EXERCISE 2

I approach the final sentences of this book with a mixture of feelings. On the one hand, I enjoy the feeling of nearing the completion of a literary quest to speak up for the ordinary. On the other hand, I know that much more could be written.

So I will leave the latter to you. My story can serve as a catalyst for your story. This book, hopefully, challenged you to appreciate more the ordinary things of life and to recognize the value of accomplishing good things that may not receive great recognition.

It goes without saying; nevertheless, I will anyway—you choose what happens next. You can choose to close this book now and place it on your shelf with your other completed written-word journeys or even post it on Amazon.com for a few bucks plus shipping.

You can also choose to take what you have learned, experienced, encountered, and highlighted (don't do that if you want "Excellent" to be the category for selling this) and live it out through speaking for, recognizing, and appreciating the good and ordinary things in your life and the lives of others. I encourage you to choose the latter.

Go live The Ordinary Way!

The End.

WORKS CITED—PART TWO

Blomberg, Craig L. *The New American Commentary*. Ed. David S. Dockery. Vol. 22 *Matthew*. Nashville: Broadman, 1992.

Bridges, Charles. *The Christian Ministry*. Edinburgh: Banner of Truth, 1997.

Bruce, F. F. *The New International Commentary on the New Testament—The Epistles to the Colossians, to Philemon, and to the Ephesians*. Grand Rapids, MI: Eerdmans, 1984.

Cathy, Truett S. *It's Easier To Succeed Than To Fail*. Nashville: Oliver-Nelson, 1989.

Cragg, Gerald. *The Interpreter's Bible*. Ed. George Arthur Buttrick. Vol.9. New York: Abingdon, 1954.

Craigie, Peter. *The New International Commentary on the Old Testament*. Ed. Harrison-Hubbard. *The Book of Deuteronomy*. Grand Rapids, MI: Eerdmans, 1976.

Curtis, David B. "Whatever Happened To Integrity." Chesapeake, VA: Berean Bible Church, 25 Feb. 2001.

Erickson, Millard J. *Concise Dictionary of Christian Theology*. Grand Rapids, MI: Baker, 1994.

Evans, Louis H., Jr. *Mastering The New Testament*. The

Communicator's Commentary Series. Ed. Lloyd J. Ogilvie, Vol. 10 Hebrews. Dallas: Word, 1985.

France, R.T. *The New International Commentary on the New Testament—The Gospel of Matthew*. Grand Rapids, MI: Eerdmans, 2007.

Goldsworthy, Graeme. *Preaching the Whole Bible as Christian Scripture*. Grand Rapids, MI: Eerdmans, 2000.

Hawkins, Tim. "Chick-fil-A." 04 June 2009 <http://www.youtube.com/timhawkinscomedy>.

Haig, Kris. "Sabbath and Spiritual Formation." *AM/FM Audio Magazine for Family Ministry*, Issue 12. CD. The Center for Family and Community Ministries, School of Social Work, Baylor University, Waco, TX. 2000.

Jacobs, A.J. *The Year of Living Biblically*. New York: Simon and Schuster, 2007.

Jenkins, David, Jr. "Anger," *Church Administration*. June 2006.

Kalland, Earl S. *The Expositor's Bible Commentary*. Ed. Frank E. Gaebelein. Vol. 3. Grand Rapids, MI: Zondervan, 1992.

King, Martin Luther, Jr. *God is Able*. Ed. Charles Henderson. 01 July 2009. <http:www. godweb.org>.

Lane, William L. *The New International Commentary on the New Testament—The Gospel of Mark*. Grand Rapids, MI: Eerdmans, 1974.

Lewis, C.S. *Mere Christianity*. New York: Collier, 1952.

Lloyd-Jones, D. Martin. *Studies In The Sermon On The Mount*. Grand Rapids, MI: Eerdmans, 1997.

McKnight, Scot. *The Real Mary*. Brewster, MA: Paraclete Press, 2007.

Miller, Calvin. *Life Is Mostly Edges*. Nashville: Thomas Nelson. 2008.

Mullins, Rich. *We Are Not as Strong As We Think We Are*. Reunion, 1996.

Park, J. Edgar. *The Interpreter's Bible*. Ed. George Arthur Buttrick. Vol.1. New York: Abingdon, 1952.

Parker, Pierson. *The Interpreter's Bible*. Ed. George Arthur Buttrick. Vol.2. New York: Abingdon, 1953.

Rylaarsdam, J. Coert. *The Interpreter's Bible*. Ed. George Arthur Buttrick. Vol.1. New York: Abingdon, 1952.

"S. Truett Cathy." *Forbes*. 31 Aug. 2015 <http://www.forbes.-com/profile/s-truett-cathy/>.

Sarna, Nahum. *Exploring Exodus*. New York: Schocken, 1996.

Schwedes, Richard. "A Wedding Sermon by Dietrich Bonhoeffer." *Lutheran Weddings* (4 Oct 2007). 05 May 2009 < http://lutheranweddings.blogspot.com>.

Shires, Henry. *The Interpreter's Bible*. Ed. George Arthur Buttrick. Vol. 2. New York: Abingdon, 1953.

Stalker, James. *Life of Christ*. Uhrichsville, OH: Barbour, 1994.

Stoddard, Drew. "'The General' Crosses The Potomac," *National Racquetball*. Vol. 14, Number 12 (1985). 13 May 2009 <http://www.rubenracquetball.com/article1.htm>.

"Take Back Your Sabbath." *Christianity Today*. (Nov. 2003).

Taylor, Barbara Brown. "Sabbath Resistance." *Christian Century*. (31 May 2005). 03 June 2009 <http://findarticles.com/p/articles/mi_m1058/is_11_122/ai_n 13806523/?tag=rbxcra.2.a.11>.

Wade, Charles. *The Jesus Principle*. Arlington, TX: Clear Stream, 2002.

Wedel, Theodore O. *The Interpreter's Bible*. Ed. George Arthur Buttrick. Vol. 10. New York: Abingdon, 1953.

Wiersbe, Warren W. Be Loyal. Colorado Springs: Chariot Victor, 1980.

Wilkins, Michael J. *The NIV Application Commentary—Matthew*. Ed. Terry Muck. Grand Rapids, MI: Zondervan, 2004.

Witherington, Ben, III. *Smyth and Helwys Bible Commentary— Matthew*. Ed. R. Scott Nash. Macon, GA: Smyth and Helwys, 2006.

Wright, G. Ernest. *The Interpreter's Bible*. Ed. George Arthur Buttrick. Vol.2. New York: Abingdon, 1953.

WORKS CITED—PART THREE

"Alaska Centenarians." Cover Story—*Alaska Dispatch News*. 28 September 2014.

Chambers, Oswald. *My Utmost For His Highest*. Ed. James Reimann. Grand Rapids: Discovery House, 1992.

Cragg, Gerald R. *The Interpreter's Bible*. Ed. George Arthur Buttrick. Vol. 9. New York: Abingdon, 1954.

Dobson, James. *Family News*. Feb. 2006. Colorado Springs: Focus on the Family.

Dowd, Alex. "Saudi Arabian Premier League Offers Daily Dose of Sportsmanship." Fox Soccer Blog. (Nov. 4, 2013) 8 Oct. 2015 <http://blog.foxsoccer.com/post/66983791736/saudi-arabian-premier-league-offers-daily-dose-of>.

Ferris, Theodore P. *The Interpreter's Bible*. Ed. George Arthur Buttrick. Vol. 9. New York: Abingdon, 1954.

Fox, Emmet. *The Sermon on the Mount*. New York: Grosset and Dunlap, 1938.

Gossip, Arthur J. *The Interpreter's Bible*. Ed. George Arthur Buttrick. Vol. 8. New York: Abingdon, 1952.

Job, Rueben P. and Norman Shawchuck. *A Guide to Prayer for Ministers and Other Servants*. Nashville: The Upper Room, 1992.

Keller, Phillip. *A Shepherd Looks at Psalm 23*. Grand Rapids: Zondervan, 1996.

Lewis, C.S. *Mere Christianity*. New York: MacMillan, 1977.

Liddell, Eric. "Thought to Apply." *Men of Integrity*. 12 May 2013.

Moo, Douglas. *The Epistle to the Romans—The New International Commentary on the New Testament*. Grand Rapids: Eerdmans, 1996.

Moo, Douglas. *Romans—The NIV Application Commentary*. Grand Rapids: Zondervan, 2000.

NPR Staff. "Ben Lecomte Swam Across The Atlantic; Next He Tries The Pacific." (23 Aug. 2015). 6 Oct. 2015 <http://www.npr.org/2015/08/23/433926565/ben-lecomte-swam-across-the-atlantic-next-he-tries-the-pacific>.

"Reasons People Don't Go To Church. Worship House Media. 06 Oct. 2015. <http://www. worshiphousemedia.com/mini-movies/20864/reasons-people-dont-go-to-church>.

Riley, William B. *Ephesians—The Threefold Epistle*. Chicago: Union Gospel Press, 1919.

Sclater, J.R.P. *The Interpreter's Bible*. Ed. George Arthur Buttrick. Vol.4. New York: Abingdon, 1955.

Snodgrass, Klyne, *The NIV Application Commentary—Ephesians*. Grand Rapids: Zondervan, 1996.

Spurgeon, Charles. *The Treasury of David*. Vol. 1. McLean, VA: MacDonald Publishing.

Stagg, Frank. *The Book of Acts*. Nashville: Broadman, 1955.

Taylor, William R. *The Interpreter's Bible*. Ed. George Arthur Buttrick. Vol.4. New York: Abingdon, 1955.

Warren, Rick. *The Purpose Driven Life*. Grand Rapids: Zondervan, 2002.

Wilson, Gerald H. *Psalms—Volume 1—The NIV Application Commentary*. Grand Rapids: Zondervan, 2002.

Wood, A. Skevington, *The Expositor's Bible Commentary*. Ed. Frank E. Gaebelein. Vol. 11. Grand Rapids: Zondervan, 1978.

WORKS CITED—PART FOUR

Shell, G. Richard. Springboard. New York: Penguin, 2013.

Works Cited—Part Six

"All Saints Church Bombing." *The Voice of the Martyrs.* Bartlesville, OK. Jan. 2014.

Blackwelder, Oscar. *The Interpreter's Bible; Galatians.* Nashville, TN; Abingdon Press. 1953.

Bock, Darrell L. *The NIV Application Commentary—Luke.* Grand Rapids, Zondervan, 1996.

Buechner, Frederick. *Wishful Thinking, A Seeker's ABC.* New York, NY. HarperCollins Publishers, 1972.

Buchanan, Mark. *Your God Is Too Safe.* Grand Rapids: Multnomah, 2001.

Buttrick, George Arthur. *The Interpreters Bible, Luke Vol. 8.* Nashville, TN: Abingdon Press, 1952

"Employee Tenure Summary." U.S. Bureau of Labor Statistics. (18 Sept. 2014). 18 July 2016

< http://www.bls.gov/news.release/tenure.nr0.htm>.

Fadling, Alan. "Someday." *Men of Integrity*. Vol. 17, No. 1, January/February 2014.

Fogelberg, Dan. "Along the Road." *Album: Phoenix*. 1979.

Geldenhuys, Norval. *The Gospel of Luke—The New International Commentary on the New Testament*. Grand Rapids: Eerdmans, 1951.

Gilmour, S. MacLean. *The Interpreter's Bible*. Ed. George Arthur Buttrick. Vol.8. New York: Abingdon, 1952.

Gladwell, Malcolm. "How I Rediscovered Faith." *Relevant Magazine*. Issue 67: Jan./Feb. 2014. 8 Jan. 2014 <http:// www.relevant-magazine.com/culture/books/how-i-rediscovered-faith#disqus_thread>.

Hansen, Kristen A. "Seasonality of Moves and Duration of Residence", U.S. Census Bureau, The Official Statistics. (1 Oct. 1998). 18 July 2016 < https://www.census.gov/sipp/p70s/p70-66.pdf>.

Hester, Dennis J. *The Vance Havner Quote Book*. Grand Rapids: Baker Book, 1986.

Hornik, Heidi J. *Attentive Patience, Christian Reflection, Vol. 58*. Waco, TX. Baylor University. 2016.

Knox, John. *The Interpreter's Bible*. Ed. George Arthur Buttrick. Vol.8. New York: Abingdon, 1952.

Luccock, Halford E. *The Interpreter's Bible*. Ed. George Arthur Buttrick. Vol.7. New York: Abingdon, 1951.

Metzger, Bruce M. and Elwyn E. Tilden. "The New Testament—Matthew." *The New Oxford Annotated Bible*. Ed. Bruce M. Metzger and Roland E. Murphy. New York: Oxford Univ. Press.

Miller, Calvin. *The Book of Jesus*. New York: Simon and Schuster, 1996.

Morris, Leon. *The Gospel According to John—The New International Commentary on the New Testament*. Grand Rapids: Eerdmans, 1995.

Ogilvie, Lloyd J. *Ask Him Anything*. Waco, TX: Word, Inc., 1981.

Peterson, Eugene. *The Message*. Colorado Springs: NavPress, 2005.

Pickert, Kate. "The Art of Being Mindful." *TIME Magazine*. February 3, 2014. 40–46.

"Purim." Judaica Guide. 10 August 2011. <http://www.judaica-guide.com/purim/>.

Singer, Thea. "The Perfect Amount of Stress—Finding Your Way to a Calmer Life." *Alaska Pulse*. January 2014. 12–14.

Tenney, Merrill C. *The Expositor's Bible Commentary*. Grand Rapids, MI, Zondervan. 1981.

Tolstoy, Leo. *Confession*. 9 Jan. < http://classicallibrary.org/tolstoy/confession/>.

Treat, Jeremy. "The Glory of the Cross. *Christianity Today*. Oct. 2013. Vol. 57, No. 8, 56–59.

Ward, William A. *ReWard Yourself*! Fort Worth Star Telegram, 1986.

Warren, Rick. *The Purpose Driven Life*. Grand Rapids: Zondervan, 2002.

"Where We Stand. Take Back Your Sabbath." *Christianity Today*. November 2003. 42–43.

WORKS CITED—PART SEVEN

Lucado, Max. *Outlive Your Life*. Nashville: Thomas Nelson, 2010.

ACKNOWLEDGMENTS

A heartfelt thanks to:

Five Stone Press – for helping bring this book to fruition.

Rabbit Creek Church – for loving your pastor.

Rabbit Creek Church pastoral team – for supporting and working with me.

Dr. Charles R. Wade – for teaching and showing me how to serve the Lord.

Carol Gilliland – for encouraging me, the countless hours of editing, typing, and your patience reading my Pentel writing.

My love to:

John T. Goodman – Dad, your dedication to God, family, and laughter inspires me. I am proud to share your middle name.

Lynn Goodman – Mom, your love, support, and patience are priceless gifts. I am so thankful for your relentless correction of my use of grammar over the years.

Loryn Hairston and Lisa Hedges – "Gils", your love for your "little" brother is evident. Thank you for letting me be "third" rather than "last".

Kate – you are beautiful inside and out. Keep dancing! Let's go get a Frosty!

Max – your determination is a gift. I want a rematch on arm wrestling!

Sam – your sense of humor delights me. Grab your cue; I'll break!

Vonda Kay – Happy 25th! Thank you for believing in me,

especially when I doubted myself. Your love and commitment are unquestioned. You amaze me!

My all to:

Jesus Christ – All things belong to You. Thank you, Lord, for seeing to it that my life is blessed by all of those people mentioned above. I pledge to live each everyday, ordinary day for You.

ABOUT THE AUTHOR

Mark T. Goodman (D. Min.) earned degrees from Baylor University, George W. Truett Seminary, and Beeson Seminary, Samford University. He serves as Senior Pastor of Rabbit Creek Church in Anchorage, Alaska and has served in vocational ministry for over twenty-eight years in Texas and Alaska.

He blogs about the subject of this book on his website marktgoodman.com and teaches biblical history and ministry courses for Wayland Baptist University. He serves annually on mission teams, serving in Alaska and abroad, including countries such as Mexico, Cambodia, Liberia, Kenya, and Thailand.

He and his wife have been married for twenty-five years and have three children, to whom they teach that they are significant as God made them to be.

Made in the USA
Middletown, DE
15 January 2023

21688707R00169